The Oculus

Unlocking the Case for Sound Money

Contents

The Cheerleaders of Doom

"Confidence in the System"

Emancipation from the Debt Plantation

Crime and Punishment

A Question of Morality

The Wealth of Nations

A Plutocratic Thugocracy

The Establishment

Corrupt and Deprave

Truth is the enemy of the State

The Monetary River System

A Small Price to Pay

The plan for total planetary domination

Nuclear Fission and the Alien Specie

Borrowing as if there's no tomorrow

El Corrida

The Diseased Currency

Banking Usury

Unlimited corruption

Child Protective Services

The Satanic Ship of State

The Question is

Molesting the Future

The Westminster Bubble

Compound Inflation

Debt and Consumption

Real Politics

State of Tyranny

Universal deceit

Control of the Press

The race to the bottom

Sub Reality

The illusion of freedom

The Church of Pounds and Pence

Modern Monetary Theory

The Magic Money Tree

The Establishment

D-Day mark2

The Yank's Folly

The Oculus, taming the Bull

Preamble

If the Universe is a great mirror of the Great Creator, his work will be reflected in those whose hearts and minds are aligned with the force of infinite love. The Bible says that God made man in his own image, therefore the divine must be seen when man reflects the teaching of the Great Creator in the purest of thoughts and actions. As humans were provided with both wisdom and free will, a polarity was also created, a choice, meaning there must be a countervailing force of unrepentant hate. That negative polarity attracts the lost, the vain and the weak, not to mention those led astray, the human condition tempted with earthborn passions, to forever torment the guilty conscience. It's never been easier to pursue such a path. The fallen ones have made it so, having signed their contract with the devil, to embrace the wickedness and revel in the destruction of mankind.

The American experience represents the ultimate fall of man. The bull has slipped its ring and is running loose, creating havoc and destruction, trashing the place, across the globe. The beast cannot be humoured into reasonable behaviour; it must be collared to contain the engorged and enraged State. Consumed by greed and loathing, the US Govt clings to its secret energy device, the source of all human suffering and malcontent, the Debt Creation and Currency Debasement. The future exploited as energy, the free energy with the ultimate cost, the children forced to pay the price of the debts created today, in compound inflation, lower real standards of living, with inevitability fewer freedoms and liberties, enslaved in an open air, rentier, debtor's prison, a hell on earth.

Considering the depths of their moral depravity and barbaric ethical transgressions, the only logical conclusion to draw is that those posing as the responsible, established order behave no better than savages. They may cloak their barbarism in fluffy liberal language but the upshot of their endeavours is systematic destruction. Their fabrications consist of crude inversions, they obscure the truth with lies, they present hate as love. The ugly is dressed up to look good in the eyes of a population that's been corrupted, robbed of discernment and abandoned critical thinking, by an "education" system designed to demoralise and misinform. Left with only surface level perception the majority cannot see the propaganda. Everything they project onto society is counterfeit, apart from the rapacious greed that motivates it. Until Govt can be returned, kicking and screaming, into a state of civilised behaviour it must wear a training aid, a gold collar, for its own good.

Time's Winged Chariot

The Chivalrous Protector of Time and Space.

Everywhere you care to look, Gold is held up as the emblematic symbol of virtue, shining bright with all the love that made it. Lady Justice holds aloft the Scales and Sword of Truth above the Old Bailey, the Orb and Sceptre is made from it, the Mace in the Commons represents its authority, the Crown is adorned with it and Gold rings clocks and watches across the land. The true importance of Gold is a closely guarded secret, not least because it exposes the Govt as a disingenuous liar and deranged fraud because where it matters most, it's nowhere to the seen.

Gold represents Sound Money and Measure, the real thing, unlike today's systematic destruction of the future by Currency Debt Creation. It represents protection from the iniquities of Debasement and evils of unrestrained Usury. Sound Money is the protector of time itself. As we hurtle through Space, a currency whose supply constantly expands distorts the space time continuum. Waves of inflation, caused by debasement, creates a black hole in the future as its energy is devoured in the present, leaving nothing but a swirling vortex of penury, tyranny and slavery.

Control over the means of exchange equates to an absolute power over the citizenry. A balance sheet of unlimited, legally enforced, resources means never having to admit being wrong. Bad decisions aren't rectified because problems can be papered over, the plaintiff's bribed and the consequences kicked into the future. Only the endemically corrupt can operate in such a moral vacuum, rippling chaos and disruption across society. When Cui Bono is applied, it's the Temple of Usury and their Corporations that thrive in such a state of moral corruption.

Gold's resurgence in fashionability reflects the collapsing currency pyramid scheme of DC and CD, the deception having been revealed resulting in naked, open air printing of worthless paper by Central Banks. The "system" is left hanging by a thread, its operatives playing Russian roulette with ticking financial nuclear fission warheads. Gold is the chivalrous protector of Earth through time and space, the truly honest regulator in nature, balancing the Divine Scales of Justice, impartial and incorruptible. Sound Money is way to venerate the past, in the present, for the future and Gold is ringing Time on this unrepentant, debauched corruption by Debt Creation and Currency Debasement.

The Counterfeiters of Love and Money

Control of the money supply has always been the apex manmade power. When real money was in use, its withdrawal from circulation could be used as a deflationary weapon on a long tern horizon of stable prices. That power is now dwarfed by the ability to create the currency, the "big bang" of unlimited debasement in an inflationary explosion of compounding legalised theft and destruction of the future. The faculty of expansion and contraction, the unbridled faux omnipotence in the face of gravity and finite limitations provided by the natural world, has appealed to despots before and the Huizi ended going for a Song. Today is no different, tyrants want tyranny to oppress and depress, to project their deranged nature in acts of wanton cruelty and corruption.

DC and CD is the American-Anglo establishment's secret source of power

It maybe inconvenient but Mob Inc and The Firm have joined forces to legalise counterfeiting and the destruction of the future. The unbridled greed and deviousness of these criminal masterminds is almost unfathomable. Savage and barbarous, it's a satanic cult of leprous sin, of double dealing child abusers, grifting for wealth and power so as to inflict pain and suffering onto humanity.

The energy they exploit is a highly guarded secret because it's so morally and ethically repugnant. The future itself has been strapped down in legal chains and ruthlessly attacked. Debt Creation and currency debasement is the American-Anglo establishment's secret power source, monetary nuclear fission, splitting the currency unit, seemingly free energy in the present if you ignore the devastating effect on the future, the children, whose energy is harvested and souls tortured in this ritual cult sacrifice. Organised as a currency pyramid scheme of created bank debts, the children are forced into the cult as a punishment for citizenship and made to work in the fields of usury picking interest and paying higher prices with increasingly lower real standards of living, freedoms and opportunities.

As with all pyramid schemes, the first participants make the ill-gotten gains and the "rewards" diminish dramatically in subsequent "generations". Started in 1971, the Babyboomers were the first largely unwitting marks and today this generation still monopolise the positions of political, media and legal power, clinging to the illusion of their probity and entrenched in denial. In just 50yrs, the new participants taking on their student debts face a rentier hell with fewer liberties in almost prison conditions, their lives are destined to be spent paying for the debts, interest and inflation created to buy the boomers ignorant acquiescence. The future is growing exponentially poorer in the real terms, leading quickly and inevitably to the situation whereby a few own everything including nation states of plantation debt slaves.

This hideous pyramid scheme offers the individual participants tiny morsels of temptation and crumbs brushed from the table, as a distraction, while prison conditions for body and mind are constructed. In today's orchestrated panic, the gates and fences of the facility are going up everywhere. From internet censorship to handheld panopticons, forced vaccinations and the chemical cosh, cameras and listening devices everywhere, people are being asked to give up their inalienable rights for the illusion of safety in a "track and trace" bio security police state. The tyranny of plantation debt slavery is here, and must be resisted. Taken to its logical conclusion, when all the people, wealth and power is controlled, the Temple of Usury elite criminal class will want to be served by chipped, semi moronic, worker droids that are remote controlled and harmless.

The organised corruption of the people

To successfully operate a confidence scheme requires the victims or "marks" to be interested in what's being offered to them and unaware that they're being deceived. As such, the Temple of Usury has been working tirelessly to cultivate society into a greedy, unthinking, brutish amorphous grey sludge, a population of morally corrupt and spiritually demoralised individuals wandering lost in the lonely desert of human experience, waiting receptively for their ideas to be provided and thoughts moulded.

This currency pyramid scheme of created debts is so harmful to the future of humanity and the planet its true nature had be disguised. Love has many counterfeits and all are used in the cradle to grave corruption process. Lust, fear, greed and loathing are encouraged and nurtured, as money is the conduit with which to slake that thirst. Desire has also been weaponised so people "love the money" that gives them access to it. Universal truth inverted, vices disguised as virtues with a counterfeit love.

The banks are creating a demand for the debts they have to sell by subtly indoctrinating and corrupting the human race. Vain, selfish, narcissists are easy prey. The media advertisers develop the lust for carnal knowledge, the marketers appeal to negative polarity and tempt out the worst traits in people. True love, selfless and beyond the vagaries of human desire, beauty and joy as one, priceless sublime virtue, pure and unconditional, the divine love of all, is not something they value or deal in.

It maybe a dark matter but Real love is priceless, limitless and free, rendering all modern "scientific" modelling flawed because they take no account of the force. The love of money is a counterfeit. It's an unhealthy, unvirtuous obsession, a dangerous and destructive vice. With a simple inversion of universal truth, society has been taught that greed is good, a vice sold as virtue, by the snakes in the Temple of Usury.

The Corruption of the State and its minions

The capo di tutti capi that controls Mob Inc and the crooked Crown needs operatives to maintain the machinery of human parasitic predation. Sociopaths and psychopaths are required to manage the exsanguination of the future's life energy to power their "wealth creation" and the enslavement of humanity. Propaganda and the distortion of reality is the perfect method, conducted through control of the media. The mainstream creates a fairground, house of mirrors, hiding knowledge and contorting truth into a comic grotesque parody. Television produces farcical alternatives realities, fiction and escape, sideshows, theatre and games, all distracting and obscuring reality. People are taught to look up to see aliens, when they're carrying around alien specie in their wallets and purses. Subtle propaganda promotes and denigrates, gently nudging the debtors into position, all the time serving the interests of the "system" and working against those of humanity. The conscious suppression of the D word and promotion of counterfeit love is transmitted around the world, the cult's terror carried over the airwaves concealed as entertainment and news, leading folk astray.

The proclivity to inflict pain and suffering is first nature to the psychopath but must be groomed into the sociopath. Private education is the ideal environment to nurture wickedness and destroy empathy in both the spear and distaff. This is done by ritual desensitisation and dehumanisation, the individual recruit is broken and rebuilt, in the glorious isolation and walled safety of a private Xanadu. It is crucial to establish the principle of elitism and the attitude that the proles are unspeakable creatures, uncouth and unwashed, lesser and deserving of their poverty, while banishing the notion that the squalor of captivity may actually be the result of one's own behaviour. The elite school system is designed to speed up development, not as enlightened beings, but as weapons of torture, disturbed and degenerate, to be used on the captive debtors on the plantation.

In most public schools the "Rule of Six" and Principle's privilege, remains the establishment's dirty little secret, the rite of passage, the catamites sworn into a silence of shame. Obsessed with "Greek love" and pederasty, this explains why the Warren Cup in the British Museum is their prized procession. The Gill statue outside Broadcasting House is a nod and a wink to the initiates nurtured by the inner circle of evil. Waning under the weight of its perversions, the corruption of the Crown has been an on-going exercise in conjunction with the money deteriorating from merely unsound specie into a vector of mass destruction.

Conclusion

Operating a currency Pyramid Scheme of unlimited created debts on a finite planet, under the influence of gravity, is incompatible with freedom and incongruous with liberty. To escape the crud, corruption and vulgar decadence of the evil empire, we must open the apothecary box for the elixir. Emancipation from plantation slavery can be achieved with a flourish of the pen. The legislators can declare a Golden Jubilee together with the restoration of Sound Money, targeting Stable Prices to protect the people and the future from the iniquities of the few. Sound Money is the elixir of life. It prevents politicians "buying time" and placating the electorate with scraps brushed from the table on which the slavers feast on their criminal debasement. Sound Money forces the ruling class to confront the monstrous structural injustices of the voters and be held accountable for their actions. It instils a culture of honour and respect that produces ripples, society becoming rich with ideas and intelligence, the human condition lifted up on the wings of honest endeavour, not pummelled into servitude and submission.

The State has become the master criminal, counterfeiting both money and love so its victims desire what their bosses, the banks, are selling, debts posing as money and hate impersonating love. The public are meticulously deceived as marks in their pyramid scheme, surrounded by a staged reality, a fictional illusion, created to uphold a blissful pretense. With its cover blown and deception revealed, the truth is now awakened from its slumber and spreading like a wildfire through the minds of the people. The crooked Crown is faced with a dilemma, fold the con or go for broke and remove the mask to reveal the true extent of its tyrannical evil. With a bit of judicious restoration, including a Jubilee and Gold Anchor, together with a back to nature movement such as William Morris and the Pre-Raphaelites, this wretched neoliberal folly can be banished to whence it came. Time's winged chariot has returned to free the Nation and restore the Age of Gold.

The Love of Money - *Having failed to learn any lessons from history, the Govt is hellbent on unlimited growth on a finite planet. Sound Money, such as a Gold Standard, is the only way to protect the planet and the future from their greed and loathing. All govt models are flawed because they don't value and cannot put a price on love. When Govt is asked to defend today's currency Pyramid Scheme of created Debts they just grunt. The calls for a Golden Jubilee are ringing out across the World.*

Love has many counterfeits. Pure love is limitless, a joy forever, to appreciate beauty without desire, an energy woven into the rich tapestry of life. The love of money is a counterfeit. It's an unhealthy, unvirtuous obsession, a dangerous, destructive vice. With a simple inversion of universal truth, society has been taught that greed is good, a vice sold as virtue, by the hissing snakes of the Temple of Usury.

The future has been made the power source by a simple inversion of universal truth, so the population willing self-harm in a state of ignorant acquiescence. To grow the debt pyramid, folk have been seduced into a love of money, the universal truth inverted. The debtors have been bombarded with propaganda from Hollywood, to video games, to gangster culture, "greed is good", "get rich or die trying", society is corrupted by design and truth subverted by a hateful counterfeiting and extortion racket.

Unlimited debt growth on a finite planet is immiscible. The love of money is a perversion. Peel away its protective layers of spin and obfuscation and the state is nothing but a front for the underworld, Mob Rule and trade in the future for profit, creating a black hole in the future which sustains the surface level illusion that passes as reality and acceptable thought.

A Den of Iniquity - *The establishment's spiral into insanity, under the spotlight of 2020, is rooted in its deviant sexual proclivities, namely its penchant for catamites. They attempt to justify their depravity with reference to the mores of Classical Antiquity, but the mental illness is all consuming, manifesting in their desire to defile the future itself with Debt Creation and Currency Debasement. For the good of the Nation, we must question the idea that all moral and ethical surety should come from such sources and declare our own independence with a golden Jubilee, a back to nature movement and Sound Money and Measure.*

***A Celestial Journey through Space and Time** - Humanity has been blessed with individual free will, the ability to choose. This is why the "powers that be" on this planet spend so much "money" and effort trying to manipulate human choices. If presented with the unadulterated truth, information pure and unsullied, humans tend to make the right choice. The banks, corporations and their Govts want people to continue abusing the future to increase their wealth and power. To keep borrowing their created debts, which debases the currency and inflates prices, digging the abyss, a black hole in the future, formed when the great polarities are disturbed, good and evil inverted so vice is presented as virtue.*

Washington Debt Creation and Dollar debasement makes the future poorer in real terms. The future is a dimension in space time, inhabited with the hopes and dreams of the today's children, the majestic union of the Distaff and the Spear manifest in flesh and blood. The poverty and pain unleashed by Washington DC today makes the future barren, dark and negative, all hope extinguished. The celestial winds begin the swirl around this low pressure vortex, the Earth succumbing to its force is sucked into its field. Satan is a shadow casting despair, death and destruction over humanity, the future fallen and enslaved, imprisoned on a modern slave ship of state, a floating debtor's prison, riddled with vice and disease.

The forces of darkness have always practiced child sacrifice. Today is no different, as avowed Satanists, the establishment have made the future the source of their wealth and power. Exponential debt growth and currency debasement creates a quickening, higher prices compounding, deepening the black hole with increasing speed. Off course and drifting into the abyss, the rudder of morality corrupted and broken, all hope appears lost, yet the indistinguishable flame continues to illuminate the gloom, the whore of Babylon recoiling from its reflection, truth piercing its lies, resonating with all the love that made it. A free will to choose is the human struggle, to fall into Satan's black hole of eternal misery or take the right path to the Kingdom of God.

Organising Poverty *- Obscured from public view, modern govt has Ways and Means to access the Bank of England's unlimited balance sheet. In the absence of Sound Money, the State has morphed from a protector of freedoms and liberties under God, into a satanic, tyrannical and coercive force, stifling and oppressing the people. Having given itself the omnipotent power to create the currency, govt has taken on the responsibility of organising poverty, through manufactured scarcity. A monetary printing press makes very problem solvable, limitless "money" available on demand, govt by the banks corporations picking the winners and losers, a chocolate fountain of wealth to enrich but only if the population are ignorant and gullible enough to use a currency which their own enslavement and the destruction of the future.*

The modern State is a machine focused on the suppression and manipulation of the people. The State is playing God and systematically dumbing down society to hide its Achilles heel in plain view. Govt is now the banker's Temple of Usury, a neoclassical folly, all façade and Doric columns, concealing the filth and squalor of a pig sty, the population cruelly farmed by the manipulation of motivations, to encourage greed, debt and consumption. The State works tirelessly to withhold knowledge and ration intelligence, reducing public discourse to a series of grunts. Through the education system and controlled media, an electric fence has been constructed around the mind, to contain a limited purview of acceptable thoughts. Disinformation and falsehoods are also used to occupy and confuse.

With Technocratic Government, the filthy swine are farmed with precision. Monitored with total surveillance, watched over by Nanny, controlled by militarised Police, chipped and pinned, sedated and vaccinated with the chemical cosh, manipulated by the best science money can buy. The State operates the farm with an iron fist of fear and regime of deception, weoponising all the vices to keep the animals minds on the job, mesmerised with televisual flashing images into a harmless state of dead eyed, mindless, unthinking. This system of organised poverty is barbarous in its savagery. Iniquitous and immoral, these satanic double dealers are hellbent on the destruction of humanity and the planet with debt creation and debasement, the future spent protecting the crimes committed today.

Degenerate Inc - Defiling the future is the establishment's passion and its weakness. Their entire system is predicated on making the children pay for the debt creation and currency debasement of today, so it's no surprise that some of these degenerates go even further. Take Trump, he's the most prolific abuser of children in presidential history. Nobody has borrowed more for the future to repay. A Govt that encourages you to abuse your own children does not have your best interests at heart. Exponential debt creation and currency debasement makes the future poorer in real terms, the children forced to pay the higher prices and accrued interest with fewer freedoms, liberties and opportunities in a rentier hell designed by the few to predate on the many. This currency pyramid scheme is morally debauched and fundamentally unsound, a modern manifestation of satanic child sacrifice. Knowing now what these vicious, malodorous predators are capable of, maybe you should remove the blindfold and see why we must restore Sound Money to proceedings.

The USS Death Star - *Planet Earth is the metaphorical Death Star, hurtling through time and space destroying itself with Debt Creation and Currency Debasement. This Galactic Ship of State is controlled by the US Military, which including droids and deep state operatives is 1.7m strong and commanded by Donald J Trump, a prolific abuser of children and registered Democrat. Either way, both candidates are hellbent on the total annihilation of the future. A Govt that encourages you to abuse your own children does not have your best interests at heart. Exponential debt creation and currency debasement makes the future poorer in real terms, the children forced to pay the higher prices and accrued interest with fewer freedoms, liberties and opportunities in a rentier hell designed by the few to predate on the many. This currency pyramid scheme is morally debauched and fundamentally unsound, a modern manifestation of satanic child sacrifice. Knowing now what these vicious, malodorous predators are capable of, maybe you should remove the blindfold and see that Trump is the most prolific child abuser in history. No President has ever borrowed more for the future to repay. It maybe inconvenient, but Donald J Trump is the commander of the Death Star, the ship of state travelling through time and space, powered by DC and subsidised insanity, hell bent on the wilful destruction of humanity and the planet itself.*

The Limoges School - *A State with a monopoly controlling the currency and media printing presses is an authoritarian regime hellbent on the enslavement of its citizens. Hard won alienable rights, freedoms and liberties are immiscible with the relentless aggrandisement of state power. Britain has descended into open tyranny and the tentacles of the state's technocracy are strangling the life out of the Nation. A medical "emergency" has be concocted and used as a weapon to bludgeon the British people in a vicious assault to relieve them of their hard won freedoms and liberties.*

The technocracy has unleashed its agents of terror to attack the minds of the enemy. Context, truth, logic and reason have been thrown to the four winds, replaced with an orchestrated campaign of threat, supposition, misinformation and doctored statistics, fashioned into a web of lies to capture the vulnerable and unthinking.   In the absence of sound money and measure, the state is the enemy of the people. If allowed to continue, a Plantation of Debt Slavery, chained and working the fields of usury, awaits the victims. The defence of human freedom is a struggle we cannot afford to lose.

*It's **Xanadu** for the few, who enjoy sumptuous gated luxury, walled off in safety from the many that are chained to the ChiCom inspired authoritarianism, as debt slaves working the pyramid plantation. The lesser* *brethren toil in the fields of usury, policed and monitored by a surveillance panopticon, sedated and culled by the medical cosh, freedoms and liberties replaced with a merciless tyranny, inalienable rights stolen by a house trained political class following the orders handed down from their master race overlords. The Gates of hell have closed on the American dream.*

The Road to Tyranny – *Britain is hurtling down the road to tyranny in a hijacked fiat omnibus. Listening to the radio the passengers are oblivious in their stupor but fascism always comes couched in liberal language. The State has had its fiat monopoly for less than 50yrs, since Bretton Woods and the end of the Gold Standard, but in the intervening period its grown fat on the endless supply of created debts, maintained by currency debasement and roaring inflation. It's gorged on the future while buying the acquiescence of bystanders with final salary pensions and other trinkets. By the wayside freedoms and liberties have been discarded to make room for more debt. The bankers grow rich on the compound interest as the monster develops its taste for power.*

Rules, regulations and endless legislation spun like a web around the Nation. As the purchasing power of the currency plummets, the future is sacrificed to inflation. Who can fathom the appeal of endless destruction to infinity? Today the State is unconsealable, a blood sucking monster with its own endless source of sustenance, the debtors of tomorrow, a ready supply of children to feed on, their souls exsanguinated in sacrifice to debt creation and currency debasement. A fiat currency regime is immiscible with freedom and liberty, not least the inalienable right to choose. As the future becomes poorer in real terms and opportunities dry up in a rentier economy, the debt slavery reveals itself. The chains of tyranny are used to stop the plantation from revolting.

The State is the antithesis of everything good. With its ritual Cremation of Care it has turned away from God and built a Baalist Temple of Usury. It is committed to the moral corruption and spiritual demoralisation of the population. Only a Nation that's lost in the labyrinth will succumb to their road to hell. I've studied Ponerology and the State's monopoly over the medium of exchange is the root of its evil. The monster is obsessed with greed and power. It grasps for evermore control in an attempt to avert the consequences of its tortuous nightmare. Only truth can penetrate its fortress of corruption. Logic and reason is a menace that must be stamped out, which is why the weapon of censorship muzzles the populous.

Those who value liberty and freedom, those who respect the future, must use the power of secession to resist the tyranny. The State will not give up its obsession so we must give up on it with a declaration of Independence from the oppression, the licentious and coercive acts of enslavement, to establish an enclave of freedom and liberty. People can vote and choose to be released from the yoke of debt slavery. With Sound Money and Measure in hand, nature's life insurance, truth will be the protector of the people, not the enemy of the State. Armed with common law and stable prices, power with the people not the banks, balance and tranquillity will lap the shores of contentment.   Sans Dieu Rein. Emancipation from the whores of Babylon and their Cult of Death.

Cooking the Books– *When modern banks lend you "money", the created debts are accounted for as assets on the balance sheet, instead of liabilities when the money was real and backed by Gold. With a swish of the pen in 1971, the entire system was turned upside down and became not only fundamentally unsound and a criminal accounting fraud but a rigged banking monopoly. The currency foisted onto an unsuspecting public today is an asset only for the banks. Instantly, established wisdom was overturned and distorted by deception. The great polarities were inverted and virtues were sacrificed to rampant, unaccountable credit expansion and currency debasement to infinity. Greed was sold as good to support the reckless lending, vice encouraged as virtue, and society morally corrupted and spiritually demoralised by design. Liability for this new "monetary pyramid scheme" was transferred from the banks to the public. The Nation has been enslaved and systematically defrauded with the criminal complicity of Govt. Profits privatised, losses* *socialised, central bank bailouts and galactic the National Debt represent the transference of losses from private to public.*

The Economics of the Magic Money Tree – *Modern Monetary Theory is so addictive it has swept across the Globe like the latest drugs craze, disturbing the minds of its victims. Unlimited currency and endless created debts, complicated by an unrestrained "whatever it takes" laissez faire approach, living for the moment with a total disregard for the future, is the numismatic equivalent of Speed laced with PCP. It's monetary amphetamine angel dust, a fast and furious hallucinating high with distorted perception and the propensity for unhinged, violent behaviour. On the street it has a language all of its own. The dealers in the banks and their touts in the media call it "Growth", not debt creation, currency debasement and the assured poverty and enslavement of the future. The tame politicians call the transactions "Investing", not borrowing. You see, the addicts must have the truth obscured, for their own good. The ravages of sustained use, rehab and mental illness are called "Climate Change" and the continued existence of the business is known as "Sustainability". At the top of this pyramid of criminal corruption, the temple bosses have grown fabulously rich. The rapid acquisition of all the real assets has morphed from a trickle up to a raging flood. "Flexibility" is* *dealerspeak for its continued unaccountability and using creative accounting everyone from the regulators to the police gets a bung and they take their end without a whimper.*

For Millennia, "power" has been a magnet for all aspiring despots and tyrants. In the past, tyrannical control was monopolised by Kings, Queens and their advisors, today it resides with the control of the currency. The power to create the "money supply" is the apex human conceived force on the planet and the greatest folly imaginable. With Global Debt to GDP approaching 400%, the legalised monopoly on debt creation means the Banking Cartel owns the entire World. If they withdraw currency from circulation, the wave of debt default would pass all the previously privately owned assets into the hands of the creditors, the banks. Operating in parallel, a degree or two removed from reality, pulling the strings, unseen yet present, the world is in the thrall of the Temple of Usury and with the Rule of Law held on a tight leash, humanity is a serf to its new Master. Unfortunately for them, their entire nefarious existence is dependent on the "marks" remaining in hoodwinked ignorance. Truth is not a commodity they deal in which is why they go to such lengths to supress it. For the few to control the many, the truth must be surrounded by a bodyguard of lies. Smoke and mirrors confuse the inquisitive and distractions tie down and occupy the inquiring mind. Debasement to infinity is a novel Tower of Babel, the devious enemy hiding in plain sight, creating a debauched and degenerate destruction of humanity in a global plantation prison system.

The Archimedes Principle *– In Classical Economics, the indebted Ship of State is governed by the Laws of Fluid Dynamics. If the vessel is overladdened and sitting below its Plimsoll line, the Nation must either get a bigger boat to displace more volume or increase the buoyancy of the Currency. This is done by decreasing its dilution, making it more "sound", thereby increasing its density. When a Country operates rationally, pursuing stable prices with sound money, limited in nature, the ship can proceed in great trim, ready and able to weather any economic conditions it may encounter.*

Since 1913, the Federal Reserve has used deception to coerce the finite, closed ecosystem of the planet onto a perilous new course. First, they constructed a neoclassical folly with fractional reserve and inflation targeting, then in 1971, they created an alternative reality, unleashing a currency Pyramid Scheme of unlimited, fiat Debts on an unknowing population. With its foundations based on Einstein's Theory of General Relativity and a constantly expanding Universe, created debts and associated currency debasement results in the deliberate manipulation of gravity and space-time.

Exponential Washington Debt Creation is a confidence scheme predicated on the notion that the future pays for the debts conjured up today. The few lifted higher by the effort and misery of the hoodwinked, successive generations becoming poorer in real terms, bearing the weight of debt and interest already created. This pyramid casts an ever darker, lengthening shadow into the future. The exponentially growing burden, created in this fantasy Modern Monetary Theory, exists in the present but their consequences form a black hole in the future which shadow existence.

To circumvent the problem of increasing deadweight and decreasing buoyancy, due to the premeditated debasement and destruction of purchasing power, the shadowcaster's tampered with natural law, inverting reality with Inflation Targeting. The public were misinformed and deceived into irrational behaviour, accepting that higher prices are a public good. This act of monumental self-harm amounts to blasting holes into space to puncture the atmosphere thereby releasing pressure and reducing the gravitational effect on the vessel below. The latest announcement to widen the scope of targeting is designed to increase "upthrust" and speed up the demolition of the future.

As the Pyramid scheme expands, the black shadow of the darkside grows and lengthens. The toxic exhaust from debt creation and currency debasement is darkest at its base. The light of life speeding through time and space, humanity back to the future aboard the celestial ship, deceived into emitting a trail of devastation, the rotations spinning a vortex, tomorrow becomes today and the shadow of darkness engulfs the planet. In the lust for power and control, this scheme of enslavement puts govt at war with the people, whose reality is purposely manipulated into a dream world, a fantasy land, to conceal the truth and obscure the invasion by this alien specie.

Plato's Ship of State *– The American Ship of State is a hijacked, nuclear powered debtor's Prison. On first inspection the vessel appears normal, a shiny façade, nice cabins for the Officer class, a bridge adorned with the latest radar and surveillance equipment transmitting propaganda to anyone who'll listen, but it's all a blissful pretence. Below deck the USS Temple Usury operates a brutal regime, citizen prisoners are chained up in paper bondage to a currency Pyramid Scheme of unlimited, created Debts, toiling without parole to produce interest and a mushroom cloud of asset price appreciation for the elites.*

Operated on the plantation model, the propulsion is provided by a monetary nuclear fission reactor. Created debts are the highly radioactive fuel and currency debasement the fission reaction. Once spent, it remains onboard heavy and toxic, building up in ever increasing amounts, Its potency diminishing, more and more fuel is required to produce less energy, weighing the ship weighed down.

To the trained eye, USS is sinking. The Plimsoll line is submerged, she sits below natural displacement, her stability is breeched, the vessel unstable and stricken. The ship cannot continue under its own steam for fear of capsizing. The fools upon the bridge continue in a blissful state of denial but he choice is simple, dump the spent fuel rods with a jubilee, or sail on for the next storm to strike and sink the entire Nation. Courage is something we never know we have until the time comes, and those who have it in the first trial cannot be assured it'll be there in the second. Americans must abandon the ill-fated ship and scupper her to the depths whence she came.

A Cold Front *- Like a thief in the night, the Govt has whipped up a storm of hysteria, hijacking a stubborn cold virus to steal inalienable rights, freedoms and liberties in the ensuing panic. The tyrannical and criminal nature of modern Govt is laid bare when you see they're operating a fundamentally unsound pyramid scheme currency of debt creation and systematic debasement. Its fascism reimagined and rebranded for the modern age, a State at war with the people, their best interests sold down the river to the banks and their Temple of Usury. Logic and reason all discarded, truth and perspective thrown to the four winds, language and statistics twisted into a weapon,* *cutting and thrusting through the consciousness of the Nation. For the few to control the many, the establishment work tirelessly to conceal truth and subdue the population, a knee on the throat of the humanity, preventing it from reaching its true potential. All hope in the future crushed, as a cold front of darkness sweeps over the Nation.*

The Cheerleaders of Doom - *The mainstream media is designed to create a weak, morally corrupt and hateful society. It sells the "narrative", a campaign of subversion to make its audience misinformed, demoralised, scared, divided, disaffected, insecure, inferior, alone, inadequate. Bombarded with their propaganda folk have become programmed to accept that the financial system is sound and working in the best interest of the people. The truth is, it's a whopping inversion to get society into the chains of modern Plantation Slavery, debt bondage. Today's fiat currency isn't backed by anything tangible other misery and the destruction of the future. These are the consequences of debt creation and currency debasement. Just look at how inalienable right, freedoms and liberties are ritually slaughtered by Govts over the last 50yrs. These fiat tokens are the currency of the Plantation, worthless and designed to be spent at the Company Store. For entertainment debtors are encouraged to play Casino Bingo on the Corporation stocks while Govt share crops its* *victims for taxes. When you can't see the chains it doesn't feel like enslavement, but make no mistake, the owners of this Plantation, the Temple of Usury, are operating a Pyramid Scheme of Debts in plain view and you are their "marks". We must rise up before they built the Prison Gates and demand a Golden Jubilee and emancipation from debt serfdom with Sound Money and Measure.*

"Confidence in the System" *– Neoliberalism is political code for the Anglo-American establishment's novel monetary monopoly confidence game. For 50yrs, the "west" has been operating a rebranded model of Plantation Slavery, the Federal Reserve running a currency pyramid scheme of unlimited, created Debts, which instantly made citizens debt slaves, forced to use a currency of persecution. The debts created out of thin air are attached by legal contract to the new slaves who work in the fields of usury, picking interest for the plantation owners. The Temple of Usury may own the Plantation but the Govt also run their own "share cropping" racket, shaking down the victims for taxes.*

In Das Kapital, Marx noted that "uncontracted time" is the ultimate source of surplus value which "capitalism" must exploit. Instead of working the slaves 12 hours a day, this currency pyramid scheme ensures the interest bearing assets work without rest. As the debts grow exponentially, debasement inflates prices in the present, mirrored by swirling black hole of debt, interest and misery in the future. The currency crop maybe just paper but it has substance which consumes the present and weighs on the future. Debtors are toiling under the whip of violence, deception and coercion to make the future poorer in real terms. Only those that are asleep get to enjoy the new American Dream.

Emancipation from the Debt Plantation *- The status quo, the narrative of acceptable thought, conceals from public illumination the establishments latest incarnation of Plantation Slavery, a modern monetary confidence game, known as the Pyramid Scheme of created Debts. This new Plantation model doesn't involve whips and chains, it wields debt bondage and legal paper to keep the slaves in lifetime of servitude, harvesting asset price inflation and interest, from the fields of usury for the owners, the Temple of Usury. The House of Windsor fronts the con, the face on the currency tokens the "marks" use to build the pyramid scheme of created debts. The "workers" are paid subsistence wages to mend fences, built surveillance towers and stock the Company Store but are forced into borrowing to survive. The mundane and menial existences of the paid debt slaves are devoid of purpose other than paying interest, building the debt pyramid and providing the plantation with new, young debtors. Those that embrace the mindless depravity are used as "celebrities"* *and "presenters" to enforce the programming and rewarded with extra pay and trinkets.*

In exchange for administering the Plantation, Govt engages in share cropping, shaking down the debtors for taxes. The job of politicians, in collusion with the media, is to keep the slaves in a state of abject ignorance, distracted and misinformed, existing in a fantasy illusion of spin and obfuscation. Attractions are constructed to capture the attention and minds of the unthinking. Television, films, the internet are designed as a box, a trap and web to contain, dumb down and sedate the modern paid debt slaves. Viewed through the prism of state education and mass media indoctrination, slavery may seem harmless fun but not only is it morally and ethically reprehensive, debt creation and currency debasement is a path that descends quickly to the destruction of the planet rendering humanity itself unnecessary. The Plantation owners are not only criminally insane but they're operating a Death Cult.

Crime and Punishment *– Debt creation and currency debasement is infinitely more damaging to society than counterfeiting or a nuclear attack. It's criminal and core Govt policy. Systematic currency debasement fuels rampant compound inflation which makes the future poorer, in real terms, and drives the economy into the hands of the rentier. It works in the interests of the banks,* *their debtors and speculators at the expense of workers, savers, renters, children and pensioners. Such a disparity of equity de-anchors society and without the islands of safety provided by sound money, the nation drifts rudderless into the abyss, on a ghost ship riven by division, resentment and deceit.*

Sound money and measure prevents govt abusing its power. It stems the fashion for preying on the weakest and political cowardice, postponing decisions and making the children pay for the systematic debasement of the currency. It makes the entire political process productive and promotes honesty. It's the mark of an intelligent, civilised society. Debt creation and currency debasement is the most audacious crime in history. It installs a manmade apex power above the system of democracy. Obscured from view but all encompassing, it controls humanity like a hidden hand, steadily acquiring all the worlds' real wealth and enslaving the population in debt servitude.

Criminal debasement is immiscible with a fair and honest society. Such a rigged system only occurs when the banks gain control of the ship. It corrupts political and public life, the official narrative becomes riddled with monstrous deceits to conceal the dirty whopping secret, the govt set to work against the interests of the majority. Debate is stifled, the market place of ideas gets dumbed down, the few supress the many and democracy is fundamentally undermined. Such power of destruction is now the State's obsession, its passion and its weakness, preciously guarded from public view. Only those suffering from Stockholm syndrome refuse to see that it's the rot at the heart of the system.

A Question of Morality *– Britain is a Fantasy Wonderland, a Willy Wonka's factory on methamphetamines. Like a chocolate river, currency gushes forth, unlimited and free, magical and sweet. The Oompa Loompa's in Govt have the machines running 24/7 on license from the Federal Reserve. Who doesn't like chocolate? Satisfying and comforting, it's largesse for everyone, in perpetuity. It's better than the everlasting Gob Stopper. Whatsmore, the Oompa Loompa's demand we "Pig Out to Help Out" on Monday's through Wednesday's. Even the lean days have become a banquet of abundance, a ballet upon the tongue. So why have management decided to ban mirrors? With such confident exuberance, animal spirits high as a kite, what could they possibly want hidden? Could it be, Chocolate is a treat to be enjoyed sparingly, gorging on it makes you fat, obese, addicted, barely able to waddle and diabetic. In such a condition, the economy's long term health would be dire. May I evacuate a small truth, I've always believed the human condition and the Planet itself loves balance. It's anatomically pleasing like the Golden Section. Sweet and sour, light and dark, good and bad, right and wrong, the great polarities exist and persist, then reality dawns. If the* *past has taught us anything, without balance, without moderation, without the wisdom to protect the future from the temptations offered in the present, excess creates inherent, structural instability. Unlimited, Debt creation and currency debasement on a finite planet is like a diet of Bailey's Irish Cream. Willy Wonka doesn't have the children's best interests at heart.*

The Wealth of Nations *- People will give up their wealth if the definition of what constitutes being "rich" is manipulated and distorted. Real wealth is an abundance of wisdom and virtue, shared and enjoyed. A rich and thriving society is immiscible with the banker's pyramid scheme. The wealth of the Nation is being systematically destroyed by the obsession with GDP growth, the banker's code for debt creation and currency debasement. The health of the county sacrificed on the altar of greed. All embracing wellbeing, shared endeavour, tranquillity, beauty and community sold down the river. Riven by greed, rich and discontent is a condition common in abject human poverty, love and joy stolen and replaced with debt and loathing. The pursuit of profit at all costs rips the heart and sinew out of the country, leaving a soulless husk, a society lost in the labyrinth, ill, wandering alone in the desert of despair, devoid of hope or opportunity, at odds with itself and doomed to fail.*

A Plutocratic Thugocracy *- Love has many counterfeits and an obsession with power and control is one of them. The State, emboldened by the Temple of Usury's unlimited balance sheet, is like a jealous, overbearing, husband. Suspicious and irrational, listening and monitoring, violent and manipulative, the instincts of the State are abusive and controlling. The British people are cowering in the corner, terrified of the thug which has unlimited funds, the police, the judges and wields extra judicial power. Committing crimes behind a veil of "national security" is like beating your wife, once the precedent is set the abuse only escalates. The best way to keep the State under control, a prophylactic to curb its desires to denude and debase, is Sound Money and Measure, to insert an overarching power to protect the people from its despicable nature and behaviour.*

The Establishment *- I've studied Ponerology and the Establishment is a world beater. Their greatest asset is a bottomless pit of hypocrisy. Operating with the ethics of plantation owners and the morality of psychopathic killers, they love to wear the mask of liberalism and play virtue signalling, back and forth across the court of public opinion, so long as it doesn't involve giving up any of their ill-gotten vices. The name of the game is nimbyism, protecting their vacuous mediocrity, power and privilege from the "great unwashed". Just scratch the veneer of* *these spivs and whores in kitten heels and loafers and you'll find their entire existence is fake. Everything from their masks, costumes, values, motivations and beliefs, they're savages with elocution lessons. The only thing they hate more than the proles is the future, which is why their passion, and their weakness, is abusing children. It's their dark, satanic secret that none dare utter in public. They worship at the Temple of Usury, a death cult of debt creation and currency debasement, which feeds on the lifeblood of the children, exsanguinating the soul and feasting on the interest, the heart and sinew ripped out of the nation, to maintain their nefarious State of corruption.*

Corrupt and Deprave - *Debt creation and currency debasement is so destructive for the future of humanity and the planet it must be concealed from its victims. Today's currency is a monetary and psychological weapon which unleashes the law of the jungle on an unsuspecting population in a conspiracy to acquire all the real wealth in the ensuing moral and spiritual panic. The good of humanity is sacrificed in pursuit of greed and power. This currency pyramid scheme of unlimited bank debts is a system of certified, criminal insanity corrupts everything in its purview. It creates perverse incentives, undermines integrity, destroys free markets and usurps capitalism. In contravention to Natural Law and the Earth's inherent limits, the answer to every problem caused by the planet's* *inherent limits becomes print more, bailout, debase, and repeat. Mistakes are compounded, bad practice is never rectified, and power to debase and destroy the future continues without consequence behind a curtain of secrecy.*

The puppet Govt, worked by the Temple of Usury, poses as a purveyor of human altruism when its actions reveal all the traits of a psychopath. The power to print, debase, enslave and destroy is in the hands of those unfit to wield it. Everything in its dominion gorges on excess, expanding its power and reach, obese govt, military protection, corporations, cronyism, rigged market, monopolies. It encourages the worst human instincts, a society built on all the vices, presented as virtues. The Temple wants to corrupt and deprave the human condition, a society dumbed down and demoralised, wandering lost without a guide, unable to distinguish right from wrong, its principles besmirched, its reputation blackened, to destroy all faith in the divine being. God's law has been inverted, vice presented as virtue, so a few can predate on the many, Humanity reduced to a savage jungle , the great polarities smudged into a ubiquitous grey sludge, creating a hell on earth.

Truth is the enemy of the State *– The real enemy of the British State is not the Russians, the Chinese or weaponised flu, it's the truth hiding in plain sight.*

Wielding the power to print limitless currency is the State's passion and its weakness. It's their most prized possession yet it must be kept secret from the public, for if they knew that Govt had the ability to end all poverty, hardship and suffering they'd demand and end to the orchestrated political inaction. Instead, the concealment of the BofE's unlimited "resources" is the grand conspiracy conducted against the people. The entire system is a facade which requires the abolition of truth. Everything they do is predicated on deceit for the preservation of this iniquity. Truth has been banished to the dark recesses of the establishment's narrative, protected by a bodyguard of lies.

The Monetary River System *– The water levels of the monetary river system are controlled from the banks by the temple money lenders. In a pure gold standard the money supply is stable, the water ebbs and flows, steady, burbling and productive like an evening on the Tweed at Norham. The more unsound the money gets the more conditions deteriorate. Fractional Reserve, limited currency debasement, brews up a storm, the waters become choppy, the journey uncomfortable and harsh, folk become desperate and cunning. A fully unhinged, unlimited pyramid scheme of created debts, systematic currency debasement, is like the Murchison Falls, a set of rapids approaching a raging waterfall, a race to the* *bottom, travellers scrambling over the bodies to survive, ruthless death and destruction, vicious and uncivilised. Today, the ship of state lies in ruins, rotten with corruption and commanded by fools high on the crack pipe of created debts. Approaching the Niagara Falls, it's about to be smashed into the hard reality of fundamentally unsound economics, the future catching up with its monumental deceits.*

A Small Price to Pay - *The breakup of the Union would be a small price to pay to free folk from the yoke of Temple Usury and their plantation principle of debt farming. The Scottish desire for independence is not borne from a longing for a hellish Marxist dystopia, it's a deep seated dissatisfaction with Westminster rule and its direction of travel. In short, it's the unsustainable trends, set in motion but never discussed, by running a pyramid scheme of created debts against the best interests of the people, which devours the present and lays waste to the future. Such a system of child sacrifice and novel debt slavery runs at odds with sound Presbyterian principles. Sturgeon has hijacked that sense of impending danger in a bid to be her own plantation owner. The source of all the problems in the country today stems from unlimited debt creation and currency debasement. From it springs every unsustainable trend proposed by Govt and its unswerving march towards a fully formed national Debtors Prison.*

***The plan for total planetary domination -** It can't be verified but conjecture on the internet suggests that the "extermination phase" of the plan for Planetary Domination has begun. The blue print has been to run a pyramid scheme of created debts to acquire all the real assets from a growing population of debtors, while secretly building a panopticon prison for humanity. I understand the "judicious acquisition" phase has been disturbed so right on cue, the purpose bred debt slaves are being told that they're a highly virulent disease and the cause of "climate change" and surplus to requirements. Slowly at first, tip toeing along and now bang, humanity is under blitzkrieg attack by a criminal technocratic tyranny, bought and paid for by the Temple of Usury.*

Run a pyramid scheme of debts to acquire all the real assets from a growing population of debtors, while secretly building a prison for humanity, including panopticon surveillance. When the theft is complete, the slaughter can begin, unleashing the bioweapon in the metaphorical gas chambers. Right on cue, the purpose bred debtors are being told that they're surplus to requirement as the cause of "climate change" and should be made to pay to save the planet. The extermination phase has begun, vaccination being the perfect cover for a sterilisation programme and medical cull. Slowly at first, tip toeing along, more virulent and deadly virus strains will be ready and waiting. Humanity is under blitzkrieg attack by a criminal technocratic tyranny, bought and paid for by the Temple of Usury. The foe is highly intelligent and extremely evil. To defeat it we must overturn its power source and install the purest, fractional reserve free, gold dome.

Nuclear Fission and the Alien Specie - *The alien specie from the Temple of Usury is a monetary parasite whose power source is the future, exsanguinating the energy of the children by debt creation and currency debasement. In less than 50yrs of this currency nuclear fission, the future is already desolate, the American dream decimated and replaced by a new slavery. Today the new debtors entering the pyramid scheme are paying off their "education" not a mortgage on a real asset. They will never own anything apart from their misery as rentier debt slaves. This plantation system is building the future a debtor's prison, forcing the children to work in the fields of usury paying the higher prices with ever lower real standards of living, not to mention freedoms and liberties. Debt creation forces the future into abject enslavement poverty, while the few acquire all the real assets. Escape is impossible though the usual channels, as the mainstream media and politics is all bought and paid for. Their sole purpose is to keep the truth from the people so humanity participates in the systematic destruction of itself. Humanity is under blitzkrieg psychological and now biological attack by a criminal technocratic tyranny run by* *the Temple of Usury. The foe is highly intelligent and extremely evil. To defeat it we must expose its power source and erect a gold dome.*

Borrowing as if there's no tomorrow, *it's no surprise that the establishment is irresponsible, cowardly and duplicitous when the BofE's balance sheet allows it to act without check or balance, compounding problems and dumping them on the future. Borrow, Debase, Bailout is the mantra of modern Govt. Unlimited debt creation on a finite planet sets in motion the forces of annihilation. It's a race to the bottom on crack, meth and pcp. As the purchasing power of the currency is systematically destroyed, prices balloon and the future made to suffer. As the drugs wear off, the solution of the politician is a bigger hit, bailout the bubble, the children will pay. Without a reckoning, actions without consequences rig the scales of justice and throw the sword of truth into the lake of fire. In contravention of natural law, this is Death Cult Nihilism, creating a World at War with itself.*

El Corrida *- The Temple's Pyramid Scheme of Debts is exhausted and panting. As a Matador, a flash of the cape and exhibitions of bravery, interspersed with some elegant passes and balletic knife work, may appear like* *extravagant showboating for the expectant patrons, but it performs a crucial function in the Corrida. Not for the faint hearted, the laboured distress cannot be heard from the sombra, the bull must be tamed, in preparation for the final act, the muerte. The true artist doesn't just rush in at the first stumble, he waits with patience and humility, for the right moment. Only when the glint dulls and the fight ebbs can the scene take on a whole new tenor. With a final thrust of the estocada, the deed is done, the beast is dragged away and the curtain falls on the divine play.*

The Diseased Currency - *The Nation is under attack by a psychological bioweapon, a currency disease, which infects its victim, the human condition, with behavioural traits more commonly found in sociopaths and psychopaths. Known in professional circles as the PSD Virus, this currency is a pyramid scheme of created debts. Losing over 2% of its value per year, its purchasing power plumbing new depths on a daily basis, these tokens represent a liability to all except the banks. Compelled by law to be infected with the disease, people are enslaved by these coercive acts of the British Govt, manifesting a stress induced serious and destructive mental illness.*

Once unleashed, the disease spreads quickly travelling via the vector of social mores and society starts to destroy itself from within. The infected show symptoms such as acute narcissism and insatiable greed, not to mention a callous disregard for the future. Many display a cruel, even sadistic, temperament, devoid of empathy. A cunning and manipulative comportment is particularly common. Most sufferers are pathological liars and inflicted with emotional shallowness. In the worst cases, individuals lose the ability to employ critical thinking and reasoned logic, resorting to obsessive compulsive desires, such as conspicuous consumption.

With the diagnosis complete and herd infection confirmed, it's no use contacting your MP to complain about the criminal insanity of Govt acting as the super-spreader. The only known prophylactic is honesty and truth. We must recognise that the debilitating condition can only be cured by restoring real money to proceedings, putting an asset back in the hands of the people and exposing Govt as a liability, a parasite, eating away at the soul of the Nation.

The Nation of *- With the debtors locked up in abject fear in the hold, Temple's Porch Monkey is steering the Nation into towering waves of debt that engulf the present, flooding in though a huge rip in the fabric of their inverted reality. The black hole in the future is filling the vacuum, a howling wind of change laying ruin to the dilapidated slave ship of state. Instead of drowning in a sea of despair, folk must hold dominion over their paper chains* *of bondage and in 2020 see that Sound Money is the way, the truth and the light. The waves shall part revealing a faithful and righteous path to the Kingdom of Plenty, a Golden Age of Liberty, Opportunity, Vitality and Equality.*

Weaponised debasement - *There was a time when counterfeiting got you locked up in the Tower, nowadays it gets you a job in the <Treasury>. Today's money is not the real thing. These pieces of paper are tokens in a Pyramid Scheme of created Debts, the root cause of all the Nation's ills and Betty Windsor is the mug fronting the con. Systemic malfeasance and organised criminality has become normalised and all encompassing. The stench of corruption has become so ubiquitous the Parliamentary shufflebums have ceased to notice. On paper the Country appears rich, in reality it's in the gutter, debasement having removed the soul, leaving a moral and spiritual wasteland of unlimited debauchery, all goodness exsanguinated by the bloodsucking parasite, the Temple of Usury.*

Invasion by Alien specie - *The manifestation, the root of all evil in the world today is the Central Banks unlimited, created debts. X is the face of evil representing its interests. The antithesis of love, this invasive currency is a* *pestilence of avarice which causes war, enslavement and penury to prosper. Sowing seeds of division it morally corrupts the nation and leaves the future in chains. Virulent in nature and spread by deception, created debts are the most poisonous fruit on the tree of usury. An idea forged in a dialogue with hell, the fallen were tempted by a power to exploit the many with a modern slave tyranny which drives humanity to its ruin. Manifest in a concept, criminal yet legal, this alien specie has invaded the Planet. With the illusion illuminated, the enemy is now powerless to resist the force of emancipation, a people united in its desire to cast the evil back into the darkness whence it came.*

Trading in the Future - *This Govt presents itself as sound, upstanding custodians, operating with principle and equity, but behind the smoke and mirrors it's committing heinous crimes. Allow me to dispel their illusion. The more debt the banks are allowed to create, the more the "money" supply is inflated. This expanding supply chases up prices, especially of things limited in nature. The costs of Compounding Inflation are borne almost entirely by the future, the children, the majority of whom will be poorer in real terms as assets fall into fewer hands. Generational theft by legal extortion is not only morally repugnant but its financial terrorism. Systematic debasement, caused by*

Debt Creation, is trading in the future for profit. (...and their sick twisted deviance)

Nation building with sound foundations – Building with Sound foundations is the cornerstone of any sustainable endeavour. Reconstructing the nation with another paper pyramid scheme of created bank debts would be a neoclassical folly. Such a monetary system benefits the few at the expense of the majority and condemns the future to penury and slavery while aiding and abetting the destruction of the natural world. It's a gleaming facade concealing a pigsty, reminiscent of Cheltenham in the Regency Period. The enlightened approach provides everyone with a stake, the power of the nation in the hands of the people, winners and losers participating in a fair race up the hill to the finish and adulation, where virtue triumphs over vice, before a joyous crowd.

Sound Money and Measure is the way, the truth and the light. Shared endeavour, honest and fungible, balanced in nature, it limits excess and rewards risk, the nuts and bolts of the pounds and pence with tensile strength, the scales of justice balanced, stable prices calibrated, ebb and flow, not boom and bust. The race to the bottom started by debasement must be banished to the dark dungeons of the mind, scrambling over the bodies replaced with the helping hand of friendship. The apex manmade power to create currency must be removed *from those least suitable and returned to the Great Creator in which we can all trust. The Planet, the People and Time itself, demand govt run back and fetch the Age of Gold.*

"Tomorrow never comes" *- The political and media class are united in a conspiracy to protect the nature of modern "money" from exposure. For if folk knew it was created out of thin air and sold as debt they'd see the State is working against their best interests. The US Govt is now a Temple of Usury run by the Federal Reserve, exploiting American citizens as marks in a Pyramid Scheme of $ debts, constantly increasing the burden, diluting and debasing the currency, inflating prices and destroying purchasing power, while piling the costs onto the future, the lives of the next generation assured to be poorer in real terms with their freedoms and liberties removed in the vice of tyranny. The more debt created the more enslaved humanity becomes, the longer it continues the bigger the deception needed to conceal it. The "status quo", "acceptable thought" is an unvirtuous spiral sucking humanity into a black hole of Debt Slavery and Destruction. Unless stopped, all the tomorrows result in the children waking up in a Debtors Prison, helpless and unnecessary, on the land their forefathers prospered as freemen. It maybe inconvenient but every breath, every step, and every decision not to expose this monstrous plan* *for total enslavement is an act of monumental self-harm, moral and spiritual suicide, making you a willing accomplice in the annihilation of the human species.*

La Serenissima *- On my first trip to the capital I discovered something so terrifying, so monstrous, that I've only just recovered. Let me tell you, London is no Serene Republic, some say the ultimate glory of man. At its foundation is a nightmarish deception that must be overturned. The establishment is a Temple of Usury built upon debt creation and currency debasement, chipping away at the future until nothing is left but a smouldering wasteland of death and destruction. At the core of this cult is a ring of institutional child abusers sacrificing the future for power and the illusion of paper wealth in the present. Churchill said truth is protected by a bodyguard of lies, the wool is being pulled over the eyes of the innocent, so evil appears good. If people had that blindfold removed they'd see the inverted reality created for them and with righteous, furious anger ransack the temple and demand the return of sound money and God.*

Age of Deceit, truth protected by lies *- Churchill famously said "truth is so precious it must be accompanied by a bodyguard of lies". Today, the bbc remain the conduit for* *those lies and misinformation but the enemy isn't the Nazi's, it's the British People. The forces of Temple Usury have captured the Nation State by stealth and deception. With control of the currency, citizens have been reduced to farmyard Debtors, corralled and deceived into a state of self-harm, whereby a pyramid scheme of created debt and currency debasement, defrauds the present and enslaves the future, time itself having been weoponsied against the interests of all but a few. If people knew they were building an open air Debtors Prison for their children, they'd rip up their paper chains and demand action to remove this reign of terror and return to the throne Sound Money and Measure.*

__The Mirror__ - With the country locked down under house arrest, people have been forced into a state of catharsis, a period of self-reflection, sat in space with time to confront the cataclysmic awfulness of modern life under Temple Usury. The mirror, the witness and tormentor of the guilty conscience, the bland and dispassionate recorder of women's vanities, trapped alone with the truth, nowhere to run or hide. Lives predicated on greed and loathing, the faux relationships, inverted realities, the fake existence spent swinging through the trees, lying, robbing and cheating, to repay the capital and interest as debtors tied up with the bondage gear of Mammon in the Temple of Usury. A time to contemplate the vacuous nature of *modern life, climbing over the bodies in a race to the bottom, to support a system of Debt Slavery and Currency Debasement which destroys the Planet and the future. No greater act of self-harm could be imagined than pursuing unlimited growth on a finite planet yet this is Govt Policy, taught in schools, programmed by television and endorsed across the media. In the final analysis, without Sound Money and Measure to ensure love trumps hate and vice is subservient to virtue, the State is operating a thinly veiled Debtors Prison, a manifestation of Hell on Earth.*

The Pyramid Scheme of created Debts and Debasement - *In less than 50yrs of a Pyramid Scheme Currency, the sound principles that made the West great have been thrown to the four winds. Driven on by greed and loathing, society is plumbing new depths predicated on making the future pay for the Debts created today. Currency debasement is a death wish. Infinite growth on a finite planet is unsustainable in nature. It's immiscible with freedom, liberty and the Constitution. As the Debt grows at exponential rates, humanity becomes an imprisoned race, locked down in a Debtors Prison, with no prospect of parole. No President in history, apart from Nixon, has done more to enslave his own people. Before it's too late, it's time to demand a Golden Jubilee.*

Debasement destroys the purchasing power of the currency driving up prices, especially those of real assets which are limited in nature. The entire scheme is predicated on making the future, the children, pay the higher prices and interest with lower real standards of living and fewer opportunities, freedoms and liberties. A Pyramid Scheme Currency is more dangerous to a country than a standing army amassing at the border. In short order it leads to the children waking up in abject slavery on the land their forefathers called a Green and Pleasant Land.

The cost of Debasement - *The reality projected by the establishment onto an unsuspecting public is a fake, a conspiracy to deceive. The key, the Claydor, to unlock the deception is found with the "money", the apex power on earth. The public are sold the lie that Created Debts are a Public Good, when they're anything but. Everything presented by govt to the people comes from the banks point of advantage. Created debts equate to currency debasement, which means general and asset price inflation. This benefits the present, at the expense of the future. The cost of debasement and ever higher prices is paid for by the children, whose real standard of living falls. The "system" is predicated on defrauding the future. The establishment are promoting a state of denial, a moral corruption and spiritual demoralisation, to defile* *honesty itself. Only a fallen population, lost in the labyrinth, will wantonly self-harm. Britain has become a state of modern slavery, beasts of burden head down and consuming, carrying the debts into the future. The interests of the banks, as promoted by Govt, are diametrically opposed to those of the people. It may be inconvenient but the British People are the enemy of the State.*

The Plantation of Debt Slavery *–On first inspection people appear have a free choice whether to get into debt but on closer inspection, the govt is using an unlimited credit card in their name. As the govt borrows more and more created for them by the banks of Temple Usury, the balance on the People's credit card continues to grow, resulting in both the state and the taxpayers wearing shackles. Owned by its creditors, the govt manages the debt plantation on behalf of the banks, manufacturing a fictional reality, a grand delusion, to hide its true state from the voters. The people are implored and coerced into joining them, told the monstrous lie that created debts and price inflation are a public good and the unvirtuous circle of deceit ensues.*

With reality inverted, vices are presented as virtues, ignorance is sold as strength and slavery becomes freedom. The indebted state inflicts its condition onto the people. The society is morally corrupted, the deceived believe the govt has their best interests in mind and join in the hunt for the greater fool. Pestilence is spread. A country operating a system of sound money never gets into such a state because unsustainable behaviour is reined in as the market adjusts the price of its valuable objet de vertu. Power is in the hands of the people not the banks and their tame govt. The true cost of today's unlimited pyramid scheme currency, the interest rate, is around -5% to -7%, such is the damage it inflicts on the future.

Today with this currency pyramid scheme of unlimited created fiat debt the state solves its indebtedness with more, constantly upping the dose. The plantation builds walls and surveillance tower, nation frogmarched down the road to the State Debtors Prison. Individuals have no free will when an omnipotent state decides to chain its citizens. Before our eyes, walls and surveillance towers are built on the plantation as it morphs into a Debtors Prison. The path of virtue is straight and paved with gold and good intentions. It leads to fairness and prosperity for all. The path of vice, paved with created debts is dark and devious winding and paved with drudgery and deceit. It leads to disease, death and the end of humanity itself.

A system of debt creation and currency debasement is predicated on making the future pay the costs of today. It is so morally repugnant it must make tyrannical use of information, knowledge and education to obfuscate its true nature. The population is given a limited hangout, they're taught to be economically illiterate. The modern education system is designed to limit intelligence and produce ignorant functioning debtors for the plantation, ravenous to consume yet too narcissistic to question reality. Once the debtor is fully indoctrinated into their life of slavery, the only dissenting voices come from the future. The silence of the lambs is therefore vital to prevent ideas of emancipation engulfing the plantation. The Temple of Usury can control the past and most of the present but not the future, the nature of the Universe abhorring its uncivilised methods. The future has been silent, or it's been that way until now.

Sleepers Awake - The entire mess is the result of debt creation and currency debasement, the pyramid scheme that poses as modern "money". The "system" is so unsound and unhealthy, there's a media blackout and govt is sworn to silence. Already in 2020, $20trn of debt "stimulus" has been created, a staggering 20% of GDP just to plug the gap left by lockdown. Even interest free it's due to be repaid, so effectively the morbidly obese American has gained another 20% in weight and is hopeless, broken and depressed. The American Debtor is expected to continue the climb to the mythical summit of mount infinity with a 20% heavier burden. Even if the American economy manages to get back on its feet, another load is waiting to be added. The system and its host are finished. US Govt is borrowing $1trn a month, the

Federal Reserve printing $25m a minute, America is on the ventilator, unable to breathe, its lifeblood ebbing away, about to see that you had to be asleep to believe in this American Dream.

Expansion and Contraction in the Song Empire *- The precedent is found in the Expansion and Contraction of the Song Dynasty. For the Planet to exist sustainably into the future, humanity must use money that's finite in nature. This symbiosis ensures balance across the space time continuum. A currency whose supply constantly expands distorts the Great Architect's natural rhythm. Inflation caused by debasement creates a black hole, the future is devoured in the present, leaving nothing but a swirling vortex of misery, inequality and suffering. The scales of justice become unbalanced, wearing through the pivot on which they turn, leading inevitably to rack and ruin. Without money that's balanced in nature, the future of the World is pain and penury.*

See the Sun rise again *- It maybe inconvenient but the established narrative of the mainstream represents a system predicated on currency debasement and the demolition of all hope in the future. Love, the most power force in the Universe, is absent from all its calculations. It* *works for the forces of hate, creating false hope, with models developed to exploit fear, greed and loathing convincing folk to self-harm and pursue unlimited growth on a finite planet. The system has an inherent hatred of humanity, perceiving people as weak, fallen creatures that deserve pain and suffering. The truth is, they're just reflecting the darkness of their own souls.*

Money, the apex manmade construction, must be Sound for humanity to flourish. It's the only way to keep the human condition in balance, respecting the future with reverence to the past. Unlimited debt growth just ensures the future is poorer in real terms, the children forced to pay the higher prices and interest with inevitably fewer opportunities, freedoms and liberties. Sound Money, limited in nature, removes perverse incentive, promotes honest govt and places power in the hands of the people. The Country is at the crossroads. Do we continue down the Road to Hell with a system predicated on Hate, or do we choose Love.

Abolition of Slavery *– For me, it is summed it up admirably with the reflection, "Ending the Pyramid Scheme of Debts, this fundamentally unsound currency, is like the fight to abolish Slavery". The parallelism is reminiscent of Gustav Klimt. The enlightenment came from France, the odious establishment cower in the corner with their indefensible position, clinging to their* *barbarous relic, morally corrupt and spiritually barren. The Temple minions plead with the debtors to stay on the path of greed and ignorance, the BBC being the modern London Society of West India Planters and Merchants, the lobby group and propagandist representing the interests of the slave owners in the Temple of Usury. In the Polis of Athens 6BC, Solon called it Seisachtheia, to "relieve the burden". Emancipation from Temple Slavery requires a Golden Jubilee, debt forgiveness or default, culminating in the restoration of Sound Money and Measure.*

Power in the hands of people - *The adage goes, "Sound money puts power in the hands of the people, unlimited currencies take it away". Fiat currencies afford the issuer omnipotent monopoly power and are incompatible with democracy, freedom and liberty. Their existence is dependent on deception, confidence is maintained by deceit. The people become the target of a State captured by the forces of usury and determined to deceive them. The events of today were always going to happen. It appears that a flu virus has been weaponised and used as cover for a Pyramid Scheme of created Debts on its last legs to remove the final vestiges of freedom and democracy to survive. Whether it's the death rates within normal parameters, the hysterical media fear, the disproportional responses or the absence of numerical comparisons, the facts on the ground point to a* *tyrannical, authoritarian power grab culminating in a new open air Debtors Prison, with homes as cells, guarded by total surveillance with the prisoners sedated and tagged, a dystopian hell, HMP Temple Usury.*

The Globalisation of Temple Usury - *The Virus of Globalism has wrought devastation on the planet. In less than half a century of Great Delusion, the globalisation of Pyramid Scheme currency has unleashed a pestilence upon the world. It has infected the minds of men with moral corruption and spiritually demoralised the women. Trust in God usurped by temptations offered from the Banker's forked tongue. With lies and deception as tools, it has dug a black hole of misery and despair in the future. Somebody has to pay the higher prices and interest caused by the debts and debasement created today. Not only does an unlimited currency make the future poorer in real terms, it drives the unrelenting destruction of the natural world. The children are sacrificed, poverty and desolation hailed as growth and progress, everything inverted, so vice appears to be virtuous.*

Only God can be trusted with the money. The Great Architect provided ample reserves of gold and silver. A license to print a currency is an abomination and immiscible with prosperity, freedom and liberty. All the country's ills are caused by the Temple Usurers' perpetual printing and debasement. It corrupts everything including language whereby the unbridled growth of greed and unrelenting destruction of nature is hailed as progress. Unlimited currency results in unlimited bailouts. The scales are never re-set, mistakes continue unrectified, society cannot pause for reflection and the world spirals into the abyss. Corporate welfare, private profit and socialised losses represent a scheme of perverse incentives, a system where only wrongdoing isn't in perpetual regression. This hateful power of destruction must be overturned.

Banking Usury - *When you go into a modern bank you're not dealing with real money, you're using currency created by selling a debt. Charging interest on what is unlimited is the very definition of usury. As more debt is created the currency supply increases, debasing what's already in circulation. This is why the purchasing power of this currency plumbs new depths on a daily basis. This is tantamount to financial terrorism, legalised theft by the Temple Usurers. Modern banks, supported by govt, are DEBT STORES, selling bondage and profiting from the misery of others. When real Money is in circulation, Debts cannot increase in a pyramidal structure because its supply is limited by nature. Lending Sound Money attracts interest because it involves transference of wealth. It's a system of inherent stability that rewards virtue and penalises vice. It protects the future from the iniquities of* *those in power, which is why this govt doesn't want you to have it.*

Unlimited corruption - *A supply of currency that's unlimited creates a planet on a crash course with itself. It disrupts natural cycles, it produces instability and stress, it stifles virtue and rewards vice, and it's unsustainable in nature. For humanity to live sustainably in nature, the money supply must be finite. This is the basis of Sound Money, a finite planet in symbiosis with the people, ebb and the flow, the weave and the weft, in balance with God's creation, protecting humans from the weakness of their condition. With time and knowledge, Sound Money will produce perfect harmony as patrons learn the ways of the light and harness the intelligence to flourish.*

Child Protective Services - *To venerate the past is considered respectful, contemplation in the present a virtue to be admired, so why is the future treated with such utter disrespect? Abusing the future is the establishment's passion and its weakness. Today's currency pyramid scheme is the most destructive force on the planet today and its predicated on making the future pay for the debts created today. Every new debt printed dilutes existing supply and represents another piece of the* *future mined out and spent in the present. As the debt grows exponentially, the future is burdened into infinity. For some the future is unknown, for others it's being used to finance a fantasy in the present. A giant pyramid of paper debts is mirrored by a pit of hell dug out of the future. The system pleads for the debtors to live the illusion today and let the children pay the consequences. The foundation of this entire scheme is a conspiracy to distort a dimension of space-time itself. The future may see ethereal but it's real and inhabited by humanity. Make no mistake, today's children are being systematically abused by the state, aided and abetted by teachers and even their parents, all accessories in a conspiracy to defraud the future.*

The Satanic Ship of State - *Nothing good is allowed to exist within the modern State. When people realise that at the heart of this post 73 "system" is child sacrifice, they cannot maintain confidence in it. The establishment have predicated their existence on making the future pay for the debts created today which debase the currency, making those without a vote or voice carry the can. It's the children that are given higher prices and interest, resulting in lower real standards of living, not to mention fewer freedoms, liberties and opportunities in this Pyramid Scheme of created, bankers Debt. The modern State is populated by the lowest of the low. Participation* *is tacit agreement, failure to condemn is implied support. The State is Satanic, stealing from the blind, abusing the innocent and exsanguinating the lifeblood of the future.*

The Question is: *Do we want to build a Golden Arch or be buried under this Pyramid Scheme of Debts. The Golden Arch vs The Paper Pyramid Scheme - Sound money and measure builds the Golden Arch, the perfect curve, a normal distribution that can sustain the health, wealth, freedom and liberty of the planet. Blinded by greed, he Paper Pyramid Scheme robs the Nation of its dignity and the children of their future.*

Molesting the future *- The key trait that lands establishment jobs is an unflinching desire to molest the future, a willingness to pile the costs of debt creation and currency debasement onto the children of the working majority that they claim to represent. Behind the mask they're more minions of usury business, hellbent on enslaving humanity in an open air debtor's Prison. If the people knew their sedated existence was predicated on defiling their own children, they'd bolt upright from that hideous nightmare and demand the return of Sound Money and Measure. It would be the very definition of* *madness to allow the same coterie that created this catastrophic climate emergency to implement a solution.*

The Westminster Bubble - *Inside the Westminster bubble, of ever higher prices, population and debt, is a state of delusion bordering on insanity. The problem is so sensitive that it's cannot be mentioned by name. Debt is a proscribed word, enforced by Chatham House rules, to keep the secret hidden from the unwitting public. A spot of campanology is only useful if it's followed by an A to the Q. Why should the next generation pay for the Debts you've created today? Remember, it was only back in 1973 when Britain could say it had the vestiges of sound money. The supply was limited by the gold standard, acting as natural brake to the banker's avarice and fractional reserve. Today, without public awareness, a pyramid scheme of unlimited created debts has been foisted on the country. Unlimited chips, created debts piled onto created debts, never to be repaid, debasing, driving up the prices, forcing the real assets into the hands at the top. It sets the present against the future, old against young, rich against poor, right against wrong, virtue against vice. It's unsustainable in every respect unless accompanied with a plan to take all our freedoms and liberties and build an open air debtors prison for humanity.*

Compound Inflation - A currency that is constantly diluted, or debased, has its purchasing power destroyed. Every time a bank creates a debt more £'s enter circulation. This increases aggregate demand causing prices to rise. Inflation compounding on inflation means that over the term of this parliament, prices are targeted to rise 13% and 30% in a decade.

Debt and Consumption - Modern Britain is a society built on created Debts and Consumption. Let's examine the true nature of this relationship. To persuade the people to partake in conspicuous consumption they must be taught to Love Greed and that Debt is Good. These foundations are an inversion of the great polarities. Britain is being morally corrupted and spiritually demoralised by design. Vice is being presented as virtue and self-harm as living. Love, the most powerful of all emotions has been abused and turned into hate, by the deceivers of Usury and their serpents. Everywhere you look, the politicians, media and marketing are blurring the lines between fiction and reality, right and wrong, virtue and vice. Even yesterday, it was announced that fictional "harry potter animals" would be displayed at the Natural History Museum. This "system", that its compulsory to support, creates total enslavement, HMP Britain Debtor's Prison, Hell on Earth.

Real Politics - *Real politics is the acceptance that the World is run by evil people intent on doing evil things to sustain the Temple of Usury and their Pyramid Scheme of unlimited, created Debts. Translated this means the West demands perpetual war to feed the veracious appetite of the Military Industrial Complex. In the final analysis, the US and UK Govts are desperate to provoke war with Iran.*

State of Tyranny - *Without the Gold Standard, the Unlimited Balance Sheets of the Central Banking Syndicate have destroyed free market capitalism and created a tyranny. No market is open for free and fair price discovery when the "banker" has unlimited chips. The Fed's balance sheet is the most destructive force on the planet today. In 2020 the world will see the state of tyranny that exists behind the disguise. The West is now an open air debtor's prison populated with mind controlled inmates experiencing a manufactured illusion. The programming, indoctrination and panopticon surveillance in this system would make the Germans blush.*

Universal deceit - *To understand the concept of deceit, one must comprehend the true nature of individuals involved. <JF Kennedy> once said "the road to hell is* *littered with paper currency" and he is right. A society predicated on spending the future today, borrowing on the backs of the children, requires the vices to be inverted so the victims accept avarice, theft and deception as virtues. Hoodwinked, Britain has just voted for another Govt of Vice, devoid of virtue, hawking the apex inversion that a currency of unlimited created debts is a public good.*

Printing currency is a mental illness, like the mother stealing from the kids piggy bank or forging the signature of her baby for an emergency loan. These Cons are hell bent on borrowing in the name of future, the innocent, those too young to vote, preying on ignorance of the parents who are easily moved by a few liberal phrases and some scraps brushed from the table. These people are the lowest of the low, despicable frauds and usurer's, they're the enemy of the people. The Country needs a Debt Jubilee and the return of Sound Money and Measure.

Control of the Press *- In journalism, discussing the nature of modern "money" is considered career suicide. Most wouldn't even know where to begin, having garnered their knowledge from the "education system", but those that do are stopped by editors and warned off. The entire world has fallen for the "monsters at the end of the garden", the myths made up to scare the children and* *control behaviour. The debtors have been taught to police themselves, to prosecute their own thought crimes and incarcerate their own ideas.*

The power of money may be able to buy newspapers, publishers and politicians but it cannot buy an open and enquiring mind, interested in truth, logic and reason. A blinkered view of the world will never suffice when a giant pyramid scheme of created bank debts looms over proceedings, that only the wilfully blind could ignore. Those that serve the "scheme", may receive privileges and better rations but they 're still building hell on earth, Debasing the future, destroying virtues and defiling humanity, creating penury the whip of usury, in a modern age of debt slavery.

The race to the bottom *- Participants in a pyramid scheme are trying to "find a greater fool", someone, anyone, to pay the higher price which allows the "mark" to pay the "interest" up to the top. This game of deception inevitably leads to the weakness, the innocent, being fleeced. A society that doesn't protect its children doesn't have a future and this is exactly what Govt policy is asking the public to do. Pile created paper debts onto created paper debts and through debasement destroying the purchasing power of the currency sending prices soaring 13% a 5yr term and 30% a decade, the vast majority becoming poorer in real terms as the costs of* *living soar. Inflation is the rate at which the future is destroyed.*

The Failed State - *The Western machine is out of balance. Connections have snapped, wires are loose and pivots swing without purpose. Forces that naturally compete like virtue and vice have been tampered with so that today the military industrial banking and corporate kleptocracy have control. - To restore the balance, doesn't require radical repairs, it needs sound money and measure and a honest govt that understands the dangers of monopoly power. The decisions needed may appear small but the resistance to them will be large.*

How does the orthodoxy get challenged when they control the media and the political parties? This was the great selling point of the BBC, but impartiality has been thrown to the four winds and only the case for debasement is allowed to be made. -Unless balance is restored, humanity will continue to fall into disrepair and the walls of the Open Air Debtors Prison will cease to be virtual. They are already building the physical 5G guard towers and if a Chi Com "social credit score" were introduced freedoms and liberties would disappear. The business of usury and the forces of vice are authoritarian and tyrannical in nature.

***Sub Reality** - The establishment encourage the debtors to exist in a sub-reality where everything is superficial, benign and harmless. It's a state of comfortable sedation, an intellectual stupor, which when entrenched is hard to break. The debtors have been reduced to grazing animals, head down and feeding. Years of "education" and "programming" have built high walls around the condition and anyone challenged their accepted thoughts and ideas, can expect to be met with resistance. Anything out of the narrow band of accepted reality elicits the fight or flight trigger response, such is the nature of this sub-reality. Above the surface, in C-Space, reality is almost a perfect inversion. Sub Level 1-5 (5: gcse level – fully programmed and brimming with false confidence borne from learnt ignorance. Level 5's cannot see the fences or surveillance equipment, they're oblivious to their enslavement 1: Corporatedebtbot – programming has been diluted by the corporate need to deceive. This can provide some contradictory triggers, emotions such as guilt, but the desire to conform in the Sub Reality overpowers any thoughts of resistance).   Without the emotional strength and intelligence to consider contradictory ideas, the electric fence of conformity can never be breached. Good citizens, productive members of society are animals in a field being farmed for profit and pleasure.*

The illusion of freedom – *Modern Slavery isn't enforced by whip and chain, it's wielded by pen and cheap legal paper. Modern slaves are debtors working under the burden of usury for the master, the banks. The rule of law allows them to operate a pyramid scheme of created debts in plain view and charge interest in the bargain. In only 40 years, it has caused the prices of real assets to soar and created a rentier economy which destroys opportunity, social mobility, freedoms and liberties while entrenching rampant inequality.*

In parallel with this enslavement, the corporate machinery of state has built the real walls of a debtor's prison. The inmates have been taught to carry tracking devices, the surveillance equipment is in every home, monitoring and listening. Super computers log and analyse every move, checking trends and learning patterns. Such technology Orwell couldn't imagine. Currently the authoritarian tyranny hides behind the curtain, watching and waiting for the time to engulf humanity. When all the debtors are safely in the technological panopticon, cashless, helpless and dependent, at the flick of the switch the virtual prisoner will have the illusion of freedom removed the cell doors will slam shut on humanity.

The Church of Pounds and Pence - Despite the Establishment pleading, the sum total of human experience cannot be valued in the pounds and pence of savage barbarism. A constantly debased, unlimited currency hides a multitude of sins, all of them concealed in the constructive ambiguity of lies, statistics and more lies. You can't put a price on Love, the highest power of all. If you try you'll soon find out it's not love at all. Govt tell the people that success is measured by GDP growth, aka Debt growth, and personal success is measured by size of the penis substitute on the driveway. Even the Church peddles the line that doing well is more important than doing good. If you measure things in the antithesis of love, it should come as no surprise that society plumbs the depths in a race to the bottom. The State, captured by the interests of fundamentally unsound money, has fallen in league with the forces of darkness and has become the enemy of the British People. Family, friendship, truth and honour don't fall into the crude purview of the banker.

House of Deceit - The entire Brexit debate was conducted under false pretences because the players allowed on stage couldn't discuss the real issues up for grabs without revealing the cataclysmic awfulness of the future being designed for us. The walls of the Open Air Debtors Prison grow higher by the day. Under cover of darkness the 5G guard towers are installed. Parliament turns a blind eye *on demand. Unlimited, unrepayable, created DEBTS cause rampant debasement and price inflation. In only 40yrs it has cause colossal inequality, the majority left languishing as rentier slaves selling their labour for a pittance. The majority have to become poorer in real terms because they have to pay the interest and higher prices of the debts accrued in the past. Allowed to continue the trend will only steepen. In another 20yrs, the working majority will be trapped in perpetual debt serfdom. All the real assets will be in hands of a decreasing few who will control, through an authoritarian technological tyranny the lives of the many. Humanity is being regressed into abject slavery before our eyes through the power of deception and silence.*

State induced mental illness *(subversion) - It maybe inconvenient but a core political and economic strategy of systematic currency debasement is so detrimental towards the future, so morally reprehensible, that in its current manifestation, the State, captured by the forces of unsound money and usury, has taken the form of a viscous, rabid predator trying to corrupt honesty itself. Using various primitive, but effective, subversion techniques, the State has been coerced into making society uninhabitable for honest, intelligent and honourable people.*

Only the morally corrupt and spiritually demoralised will pursue, with tenacity, a race to the bottom. You see, the status quo is trying to induce sickness, including mental illness, in the population. It's encouraging society to self-harm, so the broken remnants of humanity will acquiesce to full a visible enslavement in the open air debtors prison with chips, 5g panopticon surveillance, life and death controlled by the AI machine and omnipotent tyranny. Just look at China, this is the only future if this Pyramid Scheme of Debts isn't stopped.

The Golden Arch - *All intelligent people know that the medium of exchange should always reflect the nature of reality. Humanity exists under a dome, the protective layer, an enclosed ecosystem of perfection. It's limited, balanced and extremely valuable, unlike today's modern currency, the Pyramid Scheme of Debts which is unlimited, unbalanced and worthless.*

Political Hope - *Genuine "hope" is a political commodity so powerful it can change the course of Nations. Unfortunately, truth, honour and love of your fellow man are virtues that are incompatible with a fundamentally unsound currency that uses deception and debasement to achieve an illusion of prosperity.*

You see, today's Pyramid Scheme of created Debts is predicated on systematic currency debasement and an inflationary spiral to infinity. The costs of falling purchasing power and higher prices are bourne almost entirely by the future. They are expected to suffer lower real standards of living as rentier debtors, servicing the interest and higher prices accrued in the past.

Of course, they don't want you to know this, because their despicable nature is laid bare for all to see. Their keystone political and monetary strategy is predicated on getting those without a vote, the future, to pay for the debts they accumulate today. When you accept this incontrovertible truth you're forced to conclude that the State is a force for evil and the enemy of the people.

The Battle of Ideas *- It doesn't matter to me who wrote the protocols or the Bible, it's the ideas contained within that matter. It's Humanity wrestling with the great polarities, good battling evil, right triumphing over wrong and love usurping hate. A fallen few want humanity locked down in the dungeon of a debtor's prison, the life force slowly expelled, all hope for the future exsanguinated as freedom and liberty is sacrificed to usury and penury. The banking elites want to own very asset on earth and leave the previous owner chained with their unlimited, created debts. Genuine replaced with fakes. Unbeknownst to many, the Biblical Battle is raging* *in deep space and through dark matter, threatening to spill over into the physical plain. All around, the forces of darkness conceal the debt pyramid and bang the drum for War.*

The Case for free markets *- A market that can't self-correct is not a free market open for price discovery. It's a rigged game, reminiscent of the mob and organised crime. Without the ebb and flow, whereby excess is punished and probity is rewarded, vice is valued above virtue and society gets sucked down into its dominion. - Helicopter money is the epitome of such a deformity that drags humanity into the depths of Hades. Failure cannot be rewarded; nothing should be too big to fail, including the system itself, the Pyramid Scheme of Debts. With Sound Money, the Gold Arch protects humanity and the planet from the iniquity of the few.*

Human debt slavery *- As more of human activity is spent paying interest accrued in the past, the highest aspirations of mankind, art, beauty and spirituality are sacrificed on the altar of unsound money and measure. In such conditions, humanity is not free, it's a slave race in the thrall of usury. If a dispassionate observer steps back from the minutiae of life to view the mega forces at work,* *the banker's pyramid scheme of unlimited debts sets in motion a race to the bottom that's an anathema to civilised behaviour. The law of the jungle is eat or be eaten, defile or be defiled, pillage or be pillaged. Everything is dragged down by the chains of enslavement and humanity is reduced to serfdom, rentier debt chattel in the hold of a pirate ship whose destination is hell on earth.*

Control of the "money supply" affects everything in existence; nobody can escape its grasp. Infact existence itself is measured by it. The ability to expand and contract at will is an omnipotent power. Individuals, corporation and nations can be brought to heel at the tap of a keyboard. This power is unnatural, it's a human construct. Nobody of sound mind would want to wield it, but the hereditary banking syndicate acquired it through deception. Debts, piled onto debts, interest gushing upwards, prices rising and freedom falling. Without a Gold Arch to protect humanity and the planet from the iniquity of the few, the fruits of human existence will be poisoned. Left to its inevitable conclusion, in short order due to its parabolic design, one person or organisation owns everything of value.

The Future of debasement *- At this rate, another decade of debasement will leave the purchasing power of sterling down another 30%. Rent for that room in the shared* *house will be £2,500 a month and managed wage increases will leave the debtor almost destitute when all the "creditor partners" have been paid. Everything will be rationed and controlled via the mobile tracking device if you've refused the chip. Compliance will be ruthlessly enforced at the push of the button like privileges being removed by the guard. Incorrect ideas, unprescribed thoughts, reasoning above your station, may result in some special targeting from the 5G weapon panopticon, its rays coercing the victim into "reasonable behaviour".*

The life of the debt slave will be unbearable without lobotimisation, a zombie humanoid state will be preferable to the constant pain delivered by the controllers through the various devices. Growing this debt pyramid, spending the future today, creating a black hole by debasing the currency, can only persist if the population are kept financially illiterate and ignorant in total surveillance, tagged like animals in the field following the Judas goat to the slaughter. Freedoms and liberties have to be removed to keep the truth hidden in the plain view. Humanity is being marched to its death under the banner of a few neo-liberal phrases such as "progress", "inclusivity" and "growth".

The Human condition- *It maybe inconvenient but the animals in the field are treated much better than the humans in this open air debtor's prison. The herd is left* *alone to graze in the pasture, thinking its own thoughts, beholden to nobody, until the hour strikes, whereas the debtor is kept in tiny cells of acceptable thought, tortured with weaponised propaganda, flashing images are seared onto the mind like a rats devouring a face, the prisoner is punished at every turn, his actions are curtailed where ever he goes, he's tracked and monitored, the eye watches and records, judging with its deviant stare.*

The inmate is dispensed poisoned food in exchange for a few sheets of funny money, the water she drinks is laced, the air she breathes is filthy, cancers pop up from everywhere, she is injected with viruses and treated like an experiment in a petri dish. At best, the debt serf can enjoy a memorable ejaculati0n or two in an otherwise pleasure less existence, whereas the viviparous debtor may gain some brief satisfaction from breeding another victim to keep the pyramid scheme afloat.

Time has been captured and set to work against humanity. The treadmill of interest and capital repayment only speeds up the destruction of the future. We are working tirelessly to destroy ourselves in a world of fantasy make believe that's a blindfold for the cataclysmic awfulness of this enslavement. Pandering to their rigged games of politics will change nothing. All hope in the future has been extinguished and replaced with debts and interest. The system itself must be ripped down for good.

Stifling Debate - *The robustness of academic debate merely reflects the state of the currency itself. The establishment is in the usury business, operating a Pyramid Scheme of created Debts in plain sight. To conceal this from the public "marks" they use force and make-believe. Britain is an inverted, fantasy land where virtue is presented as vice. The Fourth Estate propagandists are spreading moral corruption and spiritual demoralisation so the public lose their minds in the labyrinth. Inducing mental illness in the herd is core policy.*

A lucid, thinking and observant population would never accept a currency that, through systematic debasement, sheds purchasing power at 30% a decade and leaves the future enslaved and increasingly worse off in real terms. The Q, Why doesn't the BofE target stable prices? is considered career suicide in politics and the media. Only the mentally ill will self-harm when led by Judas goats to the slaughter. Until we establish a Gold Arch that protects humanity and the planet from the iniquity of the few the deterioration will only continue apace.

I can tell you from bitter personal experience that organising the deception is surprisingly simple. The banking cartel delivers their devious scheme for humanity through the foundations and secret society networks which are then burnished by the tame journalists in their media organisations. They control the entire machinery of propaganda, its formation, production and sales. Truth is their enemy so they narrow the scope of all public discussion. This is the true extent of corruption in British life and means bbc output is tantamount to a prison broadcast.

The Slavery of Humanity - *The only people who have to ask for freedoms and liberties are slaves. In the absence of sound money, modern slavery has come in the form of debt chattel usury. In a fit of criminal insanity, under the guise of "no more boom and bust", the State stole the power to create currency from Mother Nature and decided to play God, undoing the Great Creators work. It started an unlimited pyramid scheme of created debts, a bubble of debasement and inflation for total enslavement.*

As the debt pyramid gets bigger more freedoms and liberties are removed in the name of maintaining the illusion. You see, the future cannot find out its being deceived, the next generation of debtors must lift the yoke in abject ignorance, paying for the debts created today in higher prices with lower real standards of living. It's a death wish for humanity, a simpatico suicide circle, it's a journey of serfdom, suffering and misery; it's a road to hell.

The State has become the deceiver, the inverter, prophesied in the end times. It's hate posing as love, not true love, but obsession, jealously guarding the source of its power, its life force, its unlimited, created debts. Every day the walls of the debtor's prison are built higher, 5G the latest piece in the panopticon, the past is in a Mexican standoff with the present and the future. Its economic suicide executed with a gun, a noose and a bottle of pills just for good measure.

The Power of Love - *The difference between Sound Money and today's fundamentally unsound currency is like love and hate. Lending and borrowing sound money is morally acceptable because it involves transference of real value which justifies compensation. If I lend you my gold, I no longer have it to use or spend and for that loss of capital, interest can be charged. Lending a paper debt, created out of thin air, at interest is the definition of usury.*

Today, banks transfer nothing but misery and enslavement, unlimited created debt, pay off unlimited created debts and the supply of currency grows in a pyramid scheme, debasing and debasing, inflating prices, the latest debtors become progressively poorer in real terms having to pay the interest accumulating from the past, the few lifted higher on the backs of the children of the majority.

Debasing a currency into infinity isn't without cost. The costs maybe hidden by propaganda and learnt ignorance but they're borne entirely by the future, which is enslaved in penury so the present can continue living in denial today. So, know this, everything evacuated from the state broadcasters is designed to keep you toiling away destroying the future for your own children.

This so called civilised establishment sees fit to predicate its entire monetary strategy on defrauding the future, the innocent, those without a vote in the system, getting the future to pay for the debts they create today. Could they stoop any lower? The Pirate Ship of State is morally bankrupt and corrupt to the core. Just open your eyes, it's all there in plain sight.

Westminster politics *- The political differences in Westminster are minuscule. They all support Modern Monetary Theory, (the magic money tree) which benefits the rich, old families at the expense of the working majority and the children. They merely disagree on how quickly it should be grown and the length of its shadow cast over the future.*

It's called a Magic Money Tree because it's a trick. When revealed it's just another grubby deception, a confidence game. Today's economic monetary system is predicated on the banker's magic seed, called Created Debt. It's a "reap before you sow" cash crop, literally and metaphorically.

All you have to do is convince the future to do the work for you. If you bind the future in legalese, false hope and empty promises, throw in a few liberal phrases, you can make an army of child debtors do the graft, paying the higher prices and interest with fewer freedoms and liberties which from the debasement of today.

If Labour were proposing Sound Money and a Social Conscience things would be different but they want to borrow trillions for the children to repay. They're just fighting over who controls the rackets for personal gain. None of them can be trusted to do any good for Britain now or in the future.

Dystopia *- Today in AK55, five generations of Debt Droids have been created since the death of Kennedy, the last of the elected Gentile Kings. Debt Droid 5.0 looks a lot like previous generations but having had its State programming reinforced by the Baby Boomer model this means 5.0 is especially fragile, almost vacant, all independent thought having been extinguished in the name of building the "pyramid of progress".*

Ignorant acquiescence by the debt carrying worker droids is attained by a scientific approach to indoctrination. Bombarded from the cradle with weaponised propaganda fired from state controlled black mirrors in every room, across radio frequencies, in its street furniture, billboards, the advertising on products, Big Sister controls everything through its web of watching authorities. Intellectually castrated, self-Policing droids make debt creation ruthlessly efficient.

When ignorance is recognised as strength and non-sanctioned ideas trigger horror and revulsion, the droid shuts down on hearing code words, "extremist danger ", which renders the interlocutor mute. Ideas are dangerous and must be stopped. Anyway, who can fight an invisible army that builds walls around the mind, to corral and kettle the droid into submission, so all vestiges of wisdom, every scintilla of independent thought, is stamped out and destroyed.

The Serene Republic *- Without the wisdom to resist, the establishment are experiencing the repercussions of a misguided belief in their own permanence. They attempted to wrestle the reins from God's righteous path and now the heavens are interfering to restore faith in the future. Negative rates and an inverted curve are testament that a finite world must have a finite monetary system to accompany it. Operating an open ended debt pyramid scheme in a closed ecosystem defiles the space time continuum. It plunders the future, leaving nothing but a black hole of created debts, interest and misery. Exponential debt growth hastens the shadow that mirrors it.*

When the looming darkness of a future without hope engulfs the present its inverted reality is revealed. Truth concealed by lies, flawed assumptions presented as fact, good made to appear bad. Created debt is more dangerous to humanity than a nuclear bomb because it has no half-life. To re-establish the great polarities, sound money and measure must be restored to the throne. Self-correcting, honest and true, its ebb and flow maintains the balance in nature. Moral vacuums are abhorred, past is valued equally with the future, so that man can be at one with himself, gazing at infinite love.

Life as a debt slave *- As prices are driven higher by the ever growing debt pyramid and currency debasement, it becomes impossible for the majority to live without succumbing to life incarcerated as a degenerate debtor. The children forced to take a loan for their education; the banking system bombards the victims with a myriad of inducements to borrow, and not a single representative in parliament wants to have stable prices and reduce the debt. You see, they're not your representatives at all; they represent the interests of the banks.*

When I look at the British people, I see only a flicker of hope left in them. Enfeebled, the last scintilla of independent thought is being ripped from their consciousness. Beaten down by moral corruption and spiritual demoralisation, they appear resigned to their fate. Wallowing in learnt ignorance, unthinking and easily moved by a few liberal phrases, their honesty has been corrupted to create the perfect subservient debtor. With some judicious restoration I believe we can take that flicker and coax it into a life sustaining blaze.

The Chancellor - *When a modern Treasury Secretary Chancellor says "splash the cash", they mean use the Banking Cartels unlimited balance sheet and borrow more created Debt. In the public's state of leaned ignorance this seems reasonable. Interest rates are at emergency, all-time lows and it is sold as "investing" but the fact is, this is not investment, because the Treasury, is very usury, and has no intention of ever repaying the principle borrowed, that's the job of the future, the children.*

In the economics of the madhouse, the National Debt doubled in the last decade to nearly £2tn. Such indebtedness is only sustainable if interest rates remain at all-time lows. Splashing the cash is pouring petrol onto the fire, which considering the B of E is already failing its only mandate, the 2% inflation target, would mean normalising rates which would bankrupt govt, business and households. The stated economic monetary policy of debasement and inflation is a policy of self-harm that only benefits the banks.

Borrowing your way to prosperity is a deception, it means spending the future today, as it's the children who are expected to pay the real cost in higher prices and lower standards of living. It's the act of unspeakable savage, cowardice, appealing to the greed of the enfeebled citizenry and hood winking them into self-harming, those who don't even get to vote for their enslavement. You see, without Sound Money and Measure, the interests of the Govt and the population are diametrically opposed and the State is the enemy of the people.

Modern Monetary Theory - *Let's assess the madness behind the method. It's impossible to deny that the Govt is operating a Magic Money Tree. They claim the flexibility afforded by an unlimited fiat balance sheet is the major attraction. With such power to create the currency, comes great responsibility because without limit, every denial of funds becomes ideological. In short, austerity, poverty and suffering is govt policy. Of course, their entire media machine is set up to conceal this fact. Nobody is allowed to shake the tree; nobody is supposed to know it exists. The relationship between govt and the governed has become an abusive one. As with all abusive relationships, the first step to redemption is admitting there is a problem.*

May I add, to understand the true nature of the modern political class you must concentrate on their actions, not their words. The first instinct of the unsound and dishonest individual is to deny any responsibility, to pass the buck, in this case onto the weakest, those without a vote, those unable to defend themselves, those without representation, the children. The cost of piling up interest bearing debts, never to be repaid, is borne almost entirely by the future in higher prices and lower real standards of living. If more of the future is spent paying for the debts and interest accrued today, it's not hard to see that the children will be worse off in real terms. Only the blind would vote for such a pernicious state of affairs.

The Magic Money Tree *- The magic money tree grows in an age of ignorance and moral corruption. It exists in the valley of darkness and the shadow it casts stretches far into the future, for it's the children that sustain it. They are the greater fools that the scheme feeds on, they must pay the ever higher prices in deepening penury with fewer freedoms and liberties. Usury robs the nation of its wealth which is why it must be concealed from the public.*

You see, the ability to create the currency is the power to debase, which produces inflation in prices of things that are limited in nature. Cui perdo? Who's the biggest loser from this inflation trend? A. The children, the majority of whom are born with nothing. And there you have it, govt's abusive relationship with the future laid bare, banged to rites. The unthinking are tempted by greed, vanity and peer pressure to take the paper from the tree. The paper is a loan, a debt, written in law, a contract of commitment into the future. The money tree grows on interest, fertilised with usury. The magic is the illusion that it's strong, sound and stable, completely unlike a great oak. Smoke and Mirrors are used to distract and confuse, the debtors see only what the conjurer intends, the mainstream media is polluting minds to conceal its true nature.

Paying interest on a "promise" that the cartel of bankers will keep printing and selling new currency as loans, in a never ending quest to "find a greater fool", is the very definition of usury and self-harm. In the age of real money, the promise used to entail the return of the gold but that's been inverted by the virus of debasement with evermore "counterfeit money". This unvirtuous circle is compounded by the interest accrued, that's used for more scaffolding, security and screens. Make no mistake, the planet is fallen because a currency of created debts is the forbidden fruit warned of in the Garden of Eden, sold by the devil and his little helpers. We must honour God's will and restore the age of gold.

***The establishment** - Let's examine the establishment itself. If you're prepared to eat the forbidden fruit, created debt, from the Magic Money Tree, and cast a shadow over the future, getting the children to pay for the currency created today, in higher prices, lower real standards of living with fewer freedoms and liberties, you've got to be a nasty piece of work. To get into high office you've got to do evil things behind a mask of civility. The modern state can't go broke financially, only morally, but so few understand why. The state needs to set some divine rules to keep it honest, save it from itself and its perfidious, corrupt nature. It has to limit the supply of its currency. The Golden rule, printing currency destroys the future because the inflation it causes is paid for by the children the vast majority of whom are born with nothing. A civil society would never steal from its children; create an illusion of prosperity today, which ensures the next generation will be poorer. Nothing good exists in modern govt, whilst it spreads the pestilence of fundamentally unsound currency across the land.*

***D-Day mark 2** - Our greatest triumph is yet to come. D Day mark 2 will obviously be run in reverse and will involve the emancipation from Debt Slavery, storming the defences of the Debtors Prison and recapturing the Nation from the clutches of the bankers Pyramid Scheme. Britain was captured with a few pieces of cheap legal paper,* *which the banking cartel used to make usury legal. The con, sorry judicious acquisition, was done by appealing to greed and in one fell swoop the money became unhinged and morphed into a virus that's infected the population. The future is being destroyed, the children defiled, so the feckless debtors can live in denial for another day. Unless sound money is restored to the crown, these paper chains have cast a shadow so vast that humanity will be sucked into the swirling vortex of its black hole and eternal damnation.*

The Yank's Folly - *The US are poor, literally and metaphorically. They've squandered the greatest nation on earth, swindled by the banking cartel and their latest bagman, trump. The Federal Reserve is the Yank's Folly. In only a 100 years of Temple Usury, it has destroyed the purchasing power of the $, caused two world wars and enslaved the population in debt penury. - To make matters worse, the collapse of sound money, replaced with a simple, yet hideous, Pyramid Scheme of created Debts, has sparked a social cataclysm with its moral corruption and spiritual de-moralisation spread across the land, designed to break the will of the dwindling right minded people. - Unless they remove the parasite, the future is all shadow. It's the children they expect to pay for the mistakes of today, "their sweaty haste, make the night joynt labour with the day". As for the ill-fated*

Constitution, it will be ripped to shreds in the name of "progress" and thrown to the four winds so the illusion of probity can cloud the minds of the unthinking. From my mount, I hold aloft and order thee to run back and fetch the Age of Gold.

The Oculus

Taming the Bull

The term "bull" is open to multiple interpretations. It could represent the concepts of fertility, strength, speculation or rising prices. It may also conjure up images of havoc and devastation, the Epic of Gilgamesh or child sacrifice to the Minotaur or Moloch. Alternatively, the Golden Bulls, Papal and Jubilee Bulls are decree's swinging with authority, the bulla, representing the stamp of authenticity in perpetuity. In its apex context, the Bull is the beast, the horned, cloven toed ungulate, riven with rapacious greed, a talent for destruction and a total disregard for the future. The bull is the banks worshiping in the false Temple of Usury. They're responsible for the abomination, desolation and desecration of all that is Holy, what Milton referred to in Paradise Lost, as the Fall of Humanity.

From the prophesy of Kings, the Mark of the Beast is already ubiquitous across the lands in the form of numbered bank accounts. The chip is carried on the card, mostly in the right hand and the pin is seared into the head of the victims. Today's war on cash represents the final assault in the attempted Fall of Man. With no anonymous cash transactions, only those with the mark, name or number can buy or sell. The false idol set up by the beast for the people to worship is material wealth and greed, producing the unslakeable desire for the banker's wares, its counterfeit money. The wickedness of the Temple knows no bounds, the evils of debasement and vice have corrupted their hearts and minds, coalescing into an amorphous reservoir of venomous inversion, which drips from their forked tongues, corrupting and tormenting society.

A brief history of the Papal Bull

The first Jubilee Bull was issued on February 22nd 1300 by Boniface VIII, Antiquorum habet fida relation, Clement VI decreed jubilee's should occur every 50yrs, Urban VI every 33yrs, Paul II 25yrs and the last one was John Paul II Great Jubilee 2000, Incarnationis mysterium, forgiveness of sins. With a distinct absence of virtue, all the Jubilee bulls fall short, desecrating the definition found in the Book of Leviticus for the remission of sins and universal pardon, to free slaves and prisoners and forgive all debts. In providing the post-modernist Temple of Usury an ecclesiastical license to operate, the Church of Rome is aiding and abetting the corruption of the divine. The Vatican's incitement to sin appears to be nothing more than a cynical marketing ploy for its wares. The Church of hypocrisy and ultimate betrayal has clearly been corrupted by the covetous agents of usury. The banker's Bishop of Rome is adrift having recklessly abandoned all reserve.

From the Templers to the Freemasons, the agents of usury have used secret societies to recruit and rig markets, politics and people. Built to their specifications, the modern Temple of State is a replica of Solomon's Temple, after he relinquished wisdom in pursuit of greed, wives and chariots. Built on usury, deception and corruption, it's a Death Cult worshipping Debt and Debasement. Charging interest on created debts is the very definition of usury. Making the future pay the costs of currency debasement is the very definition of fraud and coercing the public by deception into such self-harm is the very definition of corruption. The pillars of this false Temple are fundamentally unsound and must be dismantled and replaced. Sprawling collections of material wealth and earthborn passions represent the Art of Corruption at its finest. Behind a veil of secrecy, this false temple has discarded the commandments and descended into idolatry.

L'oeil-de-boeuf

The banking cartel's puppet Govt of the day clings to the rampaging bull as it commits acts of mindless destruction fuelled by debt creation and currency debasement. With barbarous savagery, the beast smashes everything of value into smithereens, including morality, purchasing power and the future of both humanity and the planet. With control over the machinery of propaganda, the public have been systematically corrupted and demoralised to manufacture an insatiable avarice, so when the temptations are offered the society at large is powerless to resist. It's never been easier to pursue an interest in material greed, practice idolatry or plumb the depths of depravity. Priceless gifts from the past have been squandered and defiled, objet d'virtue lie in pieces, concepts and ideas venerated for millennia are dismissed and discarded.

Running loose the beast has laid waste to civility, morality and the future. Everything delicate and uplifting to the human condition is trampled underfoot. Organised as a Pyramid Scheme of increasingly worthless, created Debts, the Nation is being duped into participating in the premeditated destruction of all that our forebears and universal wisdom held dear. Systematic debt creation and currency debasement is the most insidious force in the universe today, the silent weapon in a quiet war against humanity on a finite planet. The more loans the banks make, the more the currency is debased, the supply diluting the value as measured by its purchasing power. The counterfeit money is spread by business transaction infecting the hearts and minds of its victims, who are forced by law onto the carrousel of self-harm.

They say a fair exchange is no robbery but the Temple of Usury's currency pyramid scheme is a ram raid on the future, an audacious smash and grab robbery conducted in broad daylight, under cover of deception. The future, truth and beauty stolen and replaced by the bankers created debts. The real assets, those limited in nature, are taken as surety in exchange for the counterfeit, increasingly worthless, currency. It's the crime of the millennia. Time has been imprisoned and held hostage while the banks extort the debtors with usury and the future is defrauded and stolen by debasement. Everywhere it's allowed to roam the bull leaves nothing but steaming piles of misery, malfeasance and corruption.

The underworld of bankers, the state, politicians and media, dupe their marks into borrowing the increasingly worthless paper whose purchasing power is constantly destroyed by debasement. Once psychologically entrapped the debtors act as active and passive recruiters, especially of their own children, who are further misled by the education curriculums to participate in the organised fraud, enslavement and destruction by usury and asset price inflation. The more debts created by the banks increases the supply of currency in circulation, which in turn exerts pressure on the prices of real assets that are limited in nature. As the breadth of the debasement gathers pace, the benefit gushes up from below, showering the established asset owning class with paper wealth and the power to further exploit their privileged position. The entire confidence scheme revolves around leaving the children of the majority, the future of humanity, ever poorer in real terms and increasingly enslaved in a rentier prison system. In its most condensed form, the state is exploiting those without a vote, , as its primary source of energy. Its top secret, concealed behind a disguise of smoke and mirrors, but the future is ladened, chained and exsanguinated, souls captured in perpetual purgatory, a contrivance of such hate and wickedness it could only be conceived by the devil himself.

The visible force of the beast is the rate of Inflation, the trajectory of planetary destruction, the speed at which the future is decimated. The symptoms of this currency virus are mass delusion, criminal sanity and monumental self-harm. Nations are suffering from the rampaging bull of currency debasement running loose in its shops full of Chinese goods. With the help of universal state and corporate propaganda, the debtors have been taught, by deception and repetition, to believe inversions of truth, namely that compound Inflation is a public good. Targeting higher prices is an attack on the future, a stampeding policy of wanton destruction, allowing the debt pyramid to grow and the best interests of the majority to be trampled. The debtors are asleep in a state induced slumber, comatose by ubiquitous propaganda and its surface level thinking. If their gaze could be lifted from the handheld surveillance devices they would see the fences and guard towers of the new plantation. The continued existence of the con depends entirely on the deceived never seeing the deception. This is key to releasing the chains of neo-slavery and with the sleepers awake the banking cartel will be powerless to stop the emancipation and righteous Jubilee.

The purchasing power of the currency plumbs new depths on a daily basis, sinking faster than the Titanic into the

Atlantic. The wilful, systematic destruction of the currency's value is a crime that corrupts society and defrauds the future. It's financial organised crime and the very definition of weaponised usury. Hidden in plain view, behind layers of distraction and misinformation, the mob spends its time covering up the crimes of the past, while the extorting the present and defrauding the future. For the banks, this currency is treasure, to the victims it's a counterfeit good. The Banks lend increasingly worthless paper to new debtors that are coerced into borrowing ever higher nominal amounts to fund a cost of living which increases exponentially due to the debasement. The planet is being held ransom by the criminally insane, the banks are "too big to fail", and the "con" can never be revealed. This weaponised monetary fission is enforced around the world by threat of nuclear annihilation. It's State psychopathy posing as civilised behaviour. In game theory, mainstream politics is the presentation of stale mate, certain planetary destruction, the rationalisation of insanity. What passes as consensus and acceptable thought is nothing more than veiled death to humanity.

See here

The self-proclaimed civilised, liberal democracies of the West are complete frauds having been captured by a deadly silent weapon in a quite war. Debt Creation and Currency Debasement has corrupted every institution of state, including the monarchy, whose likeness is used to front the deception of humanity. Some may conclude that rehabilitating such reputations without recriminations and pitch forks maybe a task not dissimilar to that of Stalin's in Russia, but nevertheless private confessions, donning the sack cloth and ashes with a grovelling apology, maybe enough to avoid the public truth and reconciliation show trial. Forgiving those that trespass and repent is a key to any virtuous endeavour.

The Pen

People that make decisions believe in a right and wrong path, meaning they follow the Law of Great Polarities which is based on a sublime good and palpable evil. The ancient teachings say the devil works by deception, tempting and twisting by inversion. This explains how many are misguided, the Nation having been convinced to believe that created debts, greed and compound inflation are a public good when in truth they're only good for the banks and their currency pyramid deception. Creating Debts and Debasing to infinity is immiscible with a sustainable existence on a finite planet. The country needs to change course immediately. The solution is found in the Law of Moses, with a 50yr Golden Jubilee, total debt forgiveness. The bull is trapped by the pen, ready for its collar. This would pave the way for Sound Money and Measure, a Gold Collar to harness the beast for good.

A jubilee turns the tables on the Temple of Usury and sound money starts a race to the pinnacles of virtue and honest endeavour. Targeting Stable Prices provides the reins that guide the very foundation of freedom, while protecting humanity and the planet from debasement which has laid ruin to all empires. The love of money and wealth are counterfeits that must be exposed. Power invested in the hands of many, not a few, ensuring honest and responsible prosperity for all. Sound Money is a doubled headed eagle, looking both ways in balance with nature. It holds back excess and the overreaching, tyrannical nature of the State. Any concept of sustainability without Sound Money is a deluded aspiration or a wilful deception.

By the process of elimination, a solution is found a stone's throw from the hills of Rome. As a sovereign State, the Vatican has the highest legal authority, and some would say the upmost moral authority, to confront the bull without being attacked economically or militarily. With such authority comes great a responsibility, for failure to address the beast, the apex issue for humanity, is Indictment by association, Inaction is acquiescence and guilt by complicity. That's a burden the Pope alone must bear. The bells are tolling for Francis and he cannot fleeth as it were a shadow. The entire world now has a focus and can judge the nature of the Papal. The bull is penned, cornered and exhausted. Does Francis slip on the collar or will he be revealed as the beast incarnate.